CRAIG, PARK, & PAULSSON'S

Annotated Guide to the 1998 ICC Arbitration Rules

WITH COMMENTARY

W. Laurence Craig
William W. Park
Jan Paulsson

OCEANA PUBLICATIONS, INC.

International Chamber of Commerce
The world business organization

Library of Congress Cataloging-in-Publication Data

International Chamber of Commerce. International Court of Arbitration.
    [Revised rules of the ICC International Court of Arbitration]
    Annotated 1998 ICC Arbitration Rules with Commentary / by
W. Laurence Craig, William W. Park Jan Paulsson.
      p. cm.
    Includes bibliographical references and index.
    ISBN 0-379-21391-5 (alk. paper)
    1. International Chamber of Commerce. International Court of Arbitration
— Rules and practice. 2. Arbitration and award, International. I. Craig, W. Laurence (William Laurence) II. Park, William W.
III. Paulsson, Jan. IV. Title.
K2400.A48 1998
341.5'22—dc21   97-52688
                                             CIP

ABOUT THE AUTHORS:

W. Laurence Craig
Member of the Bars of New York and the District of Columbia
Avocat, Paris
A.B., Williams College; J.D., Harvard University
Doctor of Law of the University of Paris
Partner, Coudert Frères, Paris

William W. Park
Professor of Law, Boston University
Member of the Bars of Massachusetts and the District of Columbia
B.A., Yale University; J.D., Columbia University; M.A., Cambridge University
Counsel, Ropes & Gray, Boston

Jan Paulsson
Member of the Bars of Connecticut and the District of Columbia
Avocat, Paris
A.B., Harvard University; J.D., Yale University
Diplôme d'études supérieures spécialisées, University of Paris
Partner, Freshfields, Paris

The authors express their thanks to Katherine Miller, legal intern, Coudert Frères, for her assistance with the text.

TABLE OF CONTENTS

Overview of the 1998 Rules

In April 1997 the Council of the International Chamber of Commerce, the ICC's governing body, approved new ICC Rules of Arbitration to enter into effect on 1 January 1998. These Rules will apply to all ICC arbitrations commenced after that date.[1] The last comprehensive revision of the ICC arbitration rules had occurred in 1975 (a previous edition dates from 1955).[2] The new Rules are designed to remedy practical problems which had arisen in the administration of the 1975 Rules, to streamline administrative procedures which had been criticized as causing delay within the arbitral proceedings, and to respond to developments in international commercial arbitration over the last twenty years as well as to the needs of users.

The first impetus for modification came from the ICC's International Court of Arbitration, which supervises ICC arbitral proceedings and is ultimately responsible for the reliability of ICC awards.[3] In 1995, the Court brought to the attention of the ICC Commission on International Arbitration specific problems arising in the administering of the 1975 Rules which required the modification thereof.[4] It considered the problems urgent and proposed a number of specific changes to be inserted in the 1975 Rules.[5] The mission of the ICC Commission on International Arbitration is to study all developments in the field of arbitration and to coordinate with all the other ICC committees and bodies so as to make available dispute resolution services in varying fields. It is a large consultative

---

1   Article 6(1) of the 1998 Rules provides that the Rules to be applied are those in effect on the date of commencement of arbitration unless the parties have agreed otherwise.

2   The rules in effect prior to the present revision were the 1975 Rules as amended and in force as of January 1, 1988 which we refer to throughout for convenience as the "1975 Rules". The 1988 revisions were minor and were never considered to constitute a new edition of the Rules. For consideration of these limited modifications, see Stephen Bond, "Amended Rules of Conciliation and Arbitration in force as of 1 January 1988", 13 *Yearbook* 179 (1988), Volker B. Trebel, "The ICC Rules of Conciliation and Arbitration of 1988", 3 International Arbitration Report, No.4, 19 (1988), Jean Jacques-Arnaldez and Ebun Jakande, "Les Amendements Apportés au Règlement d'Arbitrage de la Chambre de Commerce Internationale (C.C.I.)", 1988 *Rev. arb.* 67.

3   Article 1 of the revised Statutes of the International Court of Arbitration (*see* Appendix I) provides that: "The function of the International Court of Arbitration of the International Chamber of Commerce (the Court) is to ensure the application of the Rules of Arbitration and of the Rules of Conciliation of the International Chamber of Commerce, and it has all the necessary powers for that purpose."

4   The second sentence of Article 3 of the 1975 Statutes provided: "It [the Court] is further entrusted, if need be, with laying before the Commission on International Arbitration any proposals for modifying the Rules of Conciliation and Arbitration of the International Chamber of Commerce which it considers necessary."

5   ICC Document No. 420/338 of 14 March 1995.

group at which 62 National Committees, members of the ICC, are entitled to be represented. National Committees of countries which have particular interests in international arbitration regularly send a number of delegates. Many of the members of the Court are also delegates to the Commission, which thus immediately benefits directly from their expertise and experience. At an ICC Arbitration Commission meeting in April 1995 many delegates expressed the view that if modifications were to be made, the occasion should be seized to make a more general revision and rreordering of the Rules. It was noted that other international arbitration institutions had recently revised or were in the process of reforming their Rules for Arbitration.[6] At the same time it was recognized that a general revision would likely take longer than the time required to study the urgent propositions of the Court.

The Commission decided to name a Working Party to study the proposals made by the Court and to consider whether they were of such an urgent nature as to require their consideration for immediate adoption by way of partial revision of the Rules. In addition, the Working Party was requested to revert to the Commission with proposals as to the further mission of the Working Party, notably with respect to the need for a general revision of the Rules.[7] The Commission named Yves Derains, a French national, and a former Secretary General of the Court of Arbitration, as Chairman of the Working Party and Stephen Bond, a U.S. national, and a former Secretary General and present member of the Court, as Vice Chairman.[8]

---

6   World Intellectual Property Organization ("WIPO") Rules of 1994; London Court of International Arbitration Rules of 1985 (Revision under consideration in 1997); American Arbitration Association International Rules of 1993 (Revision adopted on 1 April 1997).

7   ICC Document No. 420/342 of 4 October 1995, *see also* ICC Document No. 420/15/1 of 16 June 1995.

8   The Chairman of the Working Party decided at the outset that the drafting language for the Working Party should be English in view of the predominance of English in ICC arbitrations and in order rapidly to disseminate drafts of revised rules to National Committees for comment. Accordingly, while discussion within the Working Party took place at least as much in French as in English, the initial drafts of the revised rules were prepared in English. A French version was prepared, initially by the Secretary of the Commission and subsequently with the assistance of a French drafting group (chaired by Patrice Level, ICC Doc. No. 420/358 of 25 Frebruary 1997). The final version of the 1998 Rules appeared initially in English and French editions. The procedure for the preparation of the 1998 Rules differs from that of the 1975 Rules, which were drafted initially in French (primarily by Jean Robert, a French member of the Court and the Rapporteur for the Commission on International Arbitration). An English version was drafted subsequently. *See* ICC Document No. 420/179 of 25 May 1975, "The Revised ICC Rules of Arbitration", report of Me Jean Robert, Rapporteur of the ICC Commission on International Arbitration; *see also* J. Robert, "Le nouveau règlement de conciliation et d'arbitrage de la Chambre de Commerce Internationale", 1976 *Rev. arb.* 83. One of the principal drafters of the

The Working Party was made up of twenty representatives (in addition to the Chairman and Vice Chairman) from nineteen countries,[9] and was designed to be widely representative of ICC National Committees and of ICC arbitration users. The Working Party's Chairman reported to the Commission's meeting in October 1995 that an overall revision of the Rules was necessary and that the proposals for revisions put forth by the Court, while no doubt generally necessary and desirable, did not present such urgency that they could not await a general revision.[10] It was pointed out that a partial revision would likely inhibit a complete revision of the Rules for many years,[11] as it is not desirable for an international arbitration center to present different versions of its rules every few years.

In proposing a mission for the Working Party,[12] Mr. Derains stressed that there was no need to change the fundamental characteristics of the ICC Rules, namely:

i) the universality and the adaptability of the Rules to all legal systems;

ii) the existence of the Court of Arbitration;

iii) the support of ICC National Committees;

iv) the control of time limits and financial matters by the institution;

v) the use of Terms of Reference;

English translation of the 1975 Rules, Paul Gelinas, a Canadian jurist resident in Paris, and at the time the Canadian member of the Court, became Chairman of the ICC Commission on Arbitration in 1996.

9 ICC Document No. 420/343, Summary Record of Commission on International Arbitration Meeting of 19 October 1995.

10 ICC Document No. 420/341 of 15 September 1995 (report of the Working Party on the Revisions to the ICC Rules of Arbitration) commenting on the revisions proposed by the Court and presented by the Secretariat of the Commission (ICC Doc. No. 420/338)). The proposals which the Court considered particularly urgent were the addition of provisions concerning multi-party arbitration, conservatory or interim measures, and the correction or interpretation of awards.

11 *Id*, at p. 7. The position had been explained by Jan Paulsson in a letter to the United States National Committee (the U.S. Council for International Business) on 12 April 1995:

The ICC Rules need reform not only to fill huge gaps, eliminate ambiguities and eflect the practice of the past two decades, but also to present a coherent structure, topic by topic (for example, the number of often heterogeneous topics crammed into Article 2 is absurd)...in that light, I believe that the face-lift being proposed would be *counterproductive;* a small change in 1995 would remove the impetus to a sorely needed fundamental revision. We would have 1988 all over again.

12 ICC Document No. 420/342 of 4 October 1995 (report of the Working Party on the Revision of the ICC Rules of Arbitration, to the meeting of the Commission on International Arbitration of 19 October 1995, on the Working Party's Proposed Mandate).

vi) the scrutiny of awards by the Court.

As stated in its Chairman's report, the Working Party intended to make proposals for revisions of the Rules which would strive to:

i) reduce delays, particularly those occasioned by administrative procedures, such as the time between filing of a Request for Arbitration and the constitution of the tribunal;

ii) reduce unpredictability;

iii) rationalize the procedure for the payment of costs;

iv) resolve defects in the 1975 Rules, either by filling existing lacunae or remedying problems which had existed in practice;

v) meet the challenges of modern institutional arbitration.

In December 1995 a memorandum was circulated by the Commission to all National Committees for comment containing the first reflections of the Working Party as to the nature of the changes to be made to the 1975 Rules.[13] Comments were requested by the end of February 1996 so that the Working Party could take these into account prior to making proposals for approval by the Commission at its spring meeting in March 1996.

The importance of consultation with National Committees should be emphasized since it gives an idea of the many sources of input in the rules revision process. All the studies and drafts of rules were submitted to the National Committees for comment. The ICC's sixty-two National Committees represent nations throughout the world with market-based economies. They include countries with civil law, common law, and Islamic law cultures; and nations in different stages of development. The National Committees commented extensively on both general and specific proposals by the Commission and its Working Party. These comments might provide useful material for academic study as constituting a portion of the "*travaux préparatoires*" of the new Rules. (The example of the UNCITRAL Model Law comes to mind; it was drafted in consultation with many U.N. member states, and a detailed record of their comments and discussions has been published.[14]

---

13   ICC Document No. 420/344 of 28 December 1995.

14   Howard Holtzman and Joseph Neuhaus, "A Guide to the UNCITRAL Model Law on International Commercial Arbitration: Legislative History and Commentary" (1991) (1307 pages); *See also* Peter Sanders "Procedures and Practices under the UNCITRAL Rules", 27 *Am. J. Comp. Law* 453 (1979) (commentary on the UNCITRAL International Commercial Arbitration Rules).) A similar study of the contributions of the ICC National Committees study would present a comparative view of arbitration practice and procedure throughout the world and illuminate their influence on the role of arbitration institutions and the conduct of arbitral proceedings. The approach of the present annotations and commentary is not so ambitious. Its authors seek no more than to provide practitioners with a brief

The Working Party's initial reflections as to the nature of changes to be made to the Rules[15] were the subject of voluminous comments from National Committees. Based on this additional input, the Chairman of the Working Party reported to the Commission at its meeting of 21 March 1996[16] and made new recommendations and modifications to its previous proposals. The report was focused mainly on proposals for reducing delays at four stages of the arbitral process:

i) the period between filing the Request for Arbitration and transmission of the file to the arbitrators (accelerating the procedure for the constitution of the Arbitral tribunal, strengthening relationships with National Committees, simplifying the payment of the advance on costs);

ii) the period between transmission of the file to the arbitrators and entering into force of the Terms of Reference (measures to clarify the requirements of the Request and the Answer and to simplify the drawing up the Terms of Reference and its contents, conditional acceptance of new claims or counterclaims after signature of the Terms);

iii) the period between entering into force of the Terms of Reference and the final hearing (disassociating the entry into force of the Terms of Reference from the payment of the advance on costs, requiring the arbitrators to provide a provisional timetable for the proceedings at the time of preparing the Terms);

iv) the period between the final hearing and notification of the award to the parties (requiring the arbitrators to fix a date on which the proceedings would be closed, requiring that they advise the Secretary General, upon closing the proceedings, of an estimated date for submission of the draft award to the Court).

After discussion at the Commission, these proposals were developed by the Working Party into draft rules.

The Working Party also made more general proposals for reducing unpredictability and improving some defective rules. In general, it proposed a complete reorganization of the Rules so that they would be presented in a logical and chronological order, tracking the progress of the arbitral proceedings. This was intended to aid the parties in the practical use of the Rules. Both the Working Party[17] and the Commission[18] emphasized that no innovations should jeopardize

---

explanation of how the 1998 Rules differ from their predecessors, how these changes came about, and how, based on past practice, they may be expected to be applied and interpreted in the future.

15 ICC Document No. 420/344 of 28 December 1995.

16 ICC Document No. 347 of 21 March 1996.

17 ICC Document No. 420/344 of 28 December 1995 (para. 72).

18 ICC Document No. 420/343 of 19 December 1995 (summary record of Commission Meeting of 19 October 1995), also ICC Document No. 420/356 (summary record of

the adaptability of the ICC Rules to the widest range of national procedural practices. This concern was shared by the National Committees in their comments. The practical effect was that the Working Party's draft would attempt to remain within the ICC tradition: a relatively brief text setting out general principles, rather than a prolix code intended to cover in detail every possible development in the proceedings.

The Working Party pointed out that certain subjects were still under review pending further comment by National Committees. These subjects included the modification of a number of existing rules which had caused practical problems in operation over the past years (dysfunctional rules), consideration of the addition of rules for subjects not covered in the 1975 Rules but frequently found in other institutional rules and, finally, the treatment of three new rules for which a text had been proposed to the National Committees but as to which further comments were expected. These included rules on the appointment of tribunals in multi-party arbitrations, the power of arbitral tribunals to order conservatory and interim measures, and the correction and interpretation of awards.

In accordance with the decision of the Commission, the Working Party held meetings in April, July and September 1996 in Plenary Session and a drafting committee session in October. Thereafter, the Working Party transmitted a complete draft of a revision of the Rules for consideration by National Committees.[19] After receipt of National Committee comments the draft Rules were discussed at the Commission's Plenary Session of 3 December 1996. Where relevant to an understanding of the final version of the Rules, comments on these discussions are contained in the notes annotating the relevant articles. The main points which were considered controversial, and engendered considerable discussion, were:

- provisions concerning multi-party arbitration,

- the required contents of the Terms of Reference and the possibility for a party, with the authorization of the Arbitral tribunal, to make new claims outside the scope of the Terms of Reference,

- specific rules for accelerated ("fast track") arbitration,

- revision of the applicable law provision of the Rules to permit the Arbitral tribunal, in the absence of agreement by the parties, directly to apply "rules of law" it finds appropriate as opposed to designating a proper law by reference to the "rule of conflict [it] deems appropriate" as set out in the 1975 Rules.

Other issues which gave rise to spirited debate were a provision entitled "truncated tribunals" originally proposed by the Working Party, a provision

Commission Meeting of 3 December 1996).

19   ICC Document No. 420/350 of 8 October 1996, attached as an annex to ICC Document No. 420\15-15 of 8 October 1996 (the draft revised Rules).

concerning correction and interpretation of awards as originally proposed by the Court, and a suggestion for revising the Rules with respect to the language of the arbitration.

The Working Party was instructed to take into account the decisions and recommendations of the Commission and to revise the draft rules on an urgent basis. Further revisions could then be circulated to National Committees for comment with a view to adoption of recommended Rules by the Commission at a special meeting to be held on 27 February 1997. The timetable was designed so as to permit the new Rules to be adopted by the Council of the ICC at its April 1997 meeting in Shanghai, following any final comments or suggestions which might be added by the Court.

The Working Party met again in December 1996 and January 1997. A new draft of the Rules was circulated to National Committees for comment.[20] After discussion at the Commission Meeting of 27 February 1997, the draft Rules were approved by the Commission, with minor revisions, and recommended for adoption by the Council of the ICC.

It remains to be seen how much the new Rules will affect actual arbitration practice. Certainly no dramatic changes were intended. The success of the revision should be assessed in light of the modest goals of the drafters — reduction of delays, rationalization of advances on costs, increased predictability, remedying of dysfunctional rules or significant lacunae, and conformity with modern arbitration practice.

The most obvious change is the rational organization of the 35 articles of the Rules (expanded from the 26 articles of the 1975 Rules) under seven subdivisions intended to track proceedings in chronological sequence.

A. Introductory Provisions

B. Commencing the Arbitration

C. The Arbitral Tribunal

D. The Arbitral Proceedings

E. Awards

F. Costs

G. Miscellaneous

Another noticeable organizational improvement was to incorporate rules which had previously been relegated in a seemingly arbitrary manner to the Internal

---

20   ICC Document No. 420/358.

Rules of the Court. The aim has been to set down in the Arbitration Rules a full set of instructions for the conduct of arbitral proceedings, thus requiring only infrequent reference to the Internal Rules. The annotated text of the Rules, below, and even more graphically, the Conversion Tables, show how matters previously found in the Internal Rules have been incorporated into the Arbitration Rules.

Many measures adopted with the goal of reducing delays or rationalizing payments of the advance on costs are essentially intended to change administrative practice. Like the slightly altered format and organization of the Rules, their effect on the parties (other than by reduction of delays) is likely to be minimal. These provisions include:

- reducing the required contents of the Request for Arbitration and the Answer, and the required initial documentation, thus permitting succinct initiation of the arbitration proceedings if the parties so desire (Articles 4 and 5);

- empowering the Secretary General to confirm an arbitrator nominated by a party (or pursuant to agreement) when the arbitrator has filed the required statement of independence and there is no objection by the other party (thus avoiding the necessity of awaiting a Committee meeting of the Court for confirmation of such nominations) (Article 9);

- providing that the Claimant may be required to pay (without corresponding payment by the Respondent) a provisional advance on costs set by the Secretary General with a view to covering the costs of arbitration until the Terms of Reference are drawn up, and to be credited against the advance on costs fixed subsequently by the Court (thus avoiding delay in the transmission of the file to the Arbitral tribunal) (Article 30 (1));

- disassociating the payment of the advances on cost by the parties from the transmission of the file to the Arbitral tribunal and the entering into force of the Terms of Reference, thus avoiding any mechanical interruption of the arbitration by one party's failure to pay. The Secretary General may, however, after consultation with the Arbitral tribunal, direct it to suspend its work on account of non-payment of an advance on cost, thus creating an incentive for the non-defaulting party to pay the other party's share of the advance in order to avoid withdrawal of the relevant claim or counterclaim (Article 30(4));

- requiring the Arbitral tribunal at the time of drawing up the Terms of Reference, to prepare a provisional timetable to be communicated to the parties and the Court (Article 18(4)); requiring arbitrators at the time of closing the proceedings to indicate to the Secretariat an approximate date by which the award will be submitted to the Court for approval (Article 22(2)).

Many of the administrative measures to reduce delays, particularly the attempts to reduce the time between the filing of the Request for Arbitration and the constitution of the Arbitral tribunal as well as the transmission of the file to it, require action by the Secretary General and the Secretariat. While specific powers are delegated to the Secretary General for this purpose (*e.g.* approving arbitrators under limited conditions, establishing a provisional advance on costs to be paid by Claimant,[21] ordering the suspension of arbitral proceedings when an advance on costs has not been paid),[22] no fundamental redefinition of the Secretary General's role was required; nor was it necessary to reapportion tasks between the Secretary General and the Court. The Secretary General remains the officer responsible for performing the administrative functions of the Court. Although this role has taken on additional importance and difficulty with the expansion of the number of ICC arbitrations and the increase in the amounts in dispute, its fundamental characteristics are the same.

Modifications that touch the Terms of Reference were also motivated, in part, by the desire to reduce delays in the arbitral process; they may have a greater impact on how arbitral proceedings are conducted.

- The requirement of the 1975 Rules that the Terms contain a "list of the issues to be determined" has been qualified in Article 18 of the 1998 Rules by the words "unless the Arbitral Tribunal considers it inappropriate". The effect is to give discretion to the arbitrators not to set out the issues. The new language provides textual support for the practice of a number of arbitrators who avoided the formal requirement under the 1975 Rules of a list of issues by adopting a generic formula such as: "The issues to be decided are those contained in the parties' pleadings and such other issues as may arise during the proceedings." The change represents a compromise between those who saw the attempt to define the issues to be determined, at least provisionally, as an extremely important step, and those who wished to accelerate and streamline the proceedings. Some were prepared to eliminate the Terms entirely. Faced with these divergent views, the Working Party and the Commission first recommended that the Terms should contain a list of the issues only "if the Tribunal considers it appropriate." The ICC Council felt this went too far. The language finally adopted makes it a general rule that issues should be defined, but gives arbitrators discretion to omit them (for a further discussion *see* comment under Article 18, *infra*).

- Another important change eases the requirement of Article 16 of the 1975 Rules under which, absent an agreed rider to the Terms, a party could make a new claim or counterclaim only "on condition that these remain within the limits fixed by the Terms of Reference." Under Article 19 of the 1998 Rules, a party may make a claim or counterclaim outside the scope of the Terms if "it has been authorized to do so by the Arbitral tribunal, which shall have regard to the nature of such new claims or counterclaims, the stage of the arbitration and other relevant circumstances."

---

21 Article 30(1).

22 Article 30(4).

Revisions to modify existing rules which had raised problems in practice, or to fill gaps observed in the administration of ICC arbitration, include the following:

- A new article deals specifically with the constitution of arbitral tribunals when there are multiple parties and where the dispute is to be referred to a three-member tribunal (Article 10). Multiple claimants or multiple respondents are required to nominate an arbitrator jointly for confirmation by the Court. In the event that the multiple parties do not do so, an attempt will be made to achieve an agreement as to a method for the constitution of the Tribunal. Where this also fails, the Court "may appoint each member of the Arbitral Tribunal and shall designate one of them to act as chairman." This new provision in the Rules conforms to a practice that the Court had adopted, under its general powers, in reaction to the decision in the French *Dutco* case, which overturned an ICC award on the grounds that the requirement that multiple defendants must nominate an arbitrator jointly, whereas the single claimant was free to choose "his" arbitrator, violated the equality between the parties. The concept that the Court "may" appoint all three arbitrators leaves it with discretionary power to utilize other methods of appointment.[23]

- A new article (Article 23) gives the arbitral tribunal specific power to order any interim or conservatory measure it deems appropriate. This fills a gap; under the 1975 Rules, the tribunal's power was only implicit from the provision of Article 8(5) of the 1975 Rules to the effect that a party could apply to a judicial authority for interim measures "before the file is transmitted to the arbitrator, and in exceptional circumstances thereafter...". The new article also gives the arbitral tribunal the power to condition the grant of such interim measures upon the applicant's providing adequate security for the cost or damage which the measure might cause.

- The power of an arbitral tribunal to correct an award on its own initiative within 30 days of rendering an award is explicitly acknowledged. A party may within the same time period request correction or interpretation of the award (Article 29). This responds to a need which the Court had observed in a few unusual cases and for which the Court had sought solutions by reference to the general rule which provides: "In all matters not expressly

---

23 No provision is expressly made for the possibility of appointing more than three arbitrators. Article 8(1) of the Rules provides: "The disputes shall be decided by a sole arbitrator or by three arbitrators". However, Article 7(6) of the Rules, "General Provisions" in the section of the Rules entitled "The Arbitral Tribunal" states: "Insofar as the parties have not provided otherwise, the Arbitral Tribunal shall be constituted in accordance with the provisions of Article 8, 9 and 10." It thus appears that the parties could agree to a number of arbitrators exceeding three and that in that case the ordinary provisions, including Article 8 "Number of Arbitrators" and Article 10 "Multiple Parties" would not apply. The Court would apparently retain the right to confirm the arbitrators proposed and would have discretion in any event not to approve a system it found unworkable (Articles 7, 35).

provided for in these Rules, the Court and the Arbitral Tribunal shall act in the spirit of these Rules and shall make every effort to make sure that the Award is enforceable at law." (Article 26, 1975 Rules; Article 35, 1998 Rules.) The Court sought a more specific power. The power of correction or interpretation of awards is circumscribed by substantial limitations so as to prevent abuse (*see* discussion in annotated text).

- In order to prevent dilatory practices at the end of the proceedings, the Court is now given discretionary power, after the closing of the proceedings, not to replace an arbitrator who has died or who has been removed by the Court, and to permit the remaining arbitrators to issue the award (Article 12(5)). This was conceived as a necessary backstop for truly exceptional situations.

Other modifications made to conform to modern arbitration practices and to permit arbitrations to be administered effectively and expeditiously include:

- providing that where the parties have not agreed on the applicable law the arbitral tribunal shall "apply the rules of law which it determines to be appropriate" (Article 17);

- requiring that the arbitral tribunal, after having assured that the parties have had a reasonable opportunity to be heard, to "declare the proceedings closed" after which no further evidence or argument may be produced (unless requested or authorized by the arbitral tribunal) (Article 22);

- providing that the parties may agree to modify time limits set by the Rules (thus permitting *inter alia* accelerated arbitration) but that the Court has the power to extend any such time as required as to permit an arbitral tribunal or the Court to fulfil its responsibilities under the Rules (Article 32);

- providing that a party which proceeds with the arbitration without objecting to the constitution of the tribunal or to the manner in which the case is conducted will be held to have waived such objections (Article 33);

- excluding liability for arbitrators, the ICC and its institutions (Article 34).

The modifications of the 1998 Rules reflect the originally defined mission of the Working Party that the Rules should not depart from the basic concept of the 1955 and 1975 Rules: a statement of the basic principles for conducting arbitral proceedings, not a detailed manual. Partially to conform to this mission, but also in some cases because a consensus was not attained among the various ICC constituencies, a number of matters considered were not dealt with in the final version of the Rules, such as:

i) ICC Pre-arbitral Referee Rules. A proposal was made, and rejected, to provide that by agreeing to ICC arbitration the parties would also agree to the ICC Pre-arbitral Referee Rules[24] which accordingly would create a mechanism to

---

24 The Pre-arbitral Referee Rules adopted by the ICC in 1990 provide a non-judicial

deal with urgent measures required prior to the constitution of the Arbitral tribunal. It was felt that the Pre-arbitral Referee Rules which have only rarely been adopted by parties should not be imposed by a general provision.

ii) "Fast-track arbitration." A modification of the Rules to provide an optional expedited or "fast-track" arbitration procedure was considered. After mixed reactions from National Committees, the Working Party withdrew the proposed text on the grounds that an attempt to suggest such an optional regime on a pre-dispute basis "was useless for trained practitioners and dangerous for newcomers to ICC arbitration."[25] Many commentators pointed out that since an expedited arbitral regime requires substantial cooperation from the parties, it is more realistic to try to agree on the details of such a procedure after a dispute has arisen, and in view of its specific characteristics. While no specific "fast track" regime has thus been established, Article 32(1) permits the parties by agreement to modify time limits under the Rules. According to its past practice, the Secretariat will cooperate with parties to work out an appropriate fast track procedure when the parties wish to do so. Article 32(2) permits the Court to extend time limits when it is necessary to do so for the arbitral mission to be fulfilled, thus preventing the arbitration from being frustrated.

iii) Confidentiality. In view of the rapidly changing, and sometimes conflicting, development of the law in various national jurisdictions relating to confidentiality in arbitration, and the obligations of parties, witnesses and counsel in that respect, the Working Party did not deem it appropriate to attempt to define rules of confidentiality or to provide sanctions for the breach thereof. A specific provision was added, however, to confirm the arbitral tribunal's power to "take measures for protecting trade secrets and confidential information." (Article 20(7)).

iv) Distinguishing between mandatory and discretionary rules. A proposal that an article should list those provisions of the Rules which were mandatory (and which the parties could not, by agreement, dispense with) and those which were discretionary could not generate consensus. The extent to which parties may "opt out" of certain provisions of the Rules is left to the discretion of the Court. The general thrust of the Rules, however, is to respect the parties' agreement as to methods of appointment of arbitrators and procedural matters, subject to the inviolability of basic elements of ICC arbitration procedure (*e.g.* the Court's power to scrutinize awards pursuant to Article 27).

---

mechanism permitting a neutral third party to order provisional relief on an urgent basis prior to determination of the merits of the dispute by the arbitral or judicial body having jurisdiction. *See* Craig, Park & Paulsson, International Chamber of Commerce Arbitration, 2d ed. 1990, Sec. 38.03.

25 Working Party on the Revision of the ICC Rules of Arbitration, Note to National Committees, ICC Doc. No. 420\358 attached to ICC Doc. No. 420\355 of 13 January 1997.

At its meeting on 27 February 1997, the ICC Arbitration Commission completed its mission by approving, subject to minor drafting revisions, a draft text of the new Rules. The draft was considered again by the Court which assisted in drafting technical revisions. The Court did not favor the Commission's recommended text for Article 18(d) of the Rules (which would have provided that the Terms would be required to contain a list of issues only "if the Arbitral Tribunal considers it appropriate"); nor did it favor Article 34 on exclusion of liability, which contained a blanket exclusion of liability not only for arbitrators in the exercise of their quasi-judicial functions but also for the ICC and its institutions, employees and members involved in the administration and supervision of arbitrations. These issues therefore were left for decision by the ICC Council to which the draft was presented at its April 1997 meeting by Robert Briner,[26] the president of the ICC International Court of Arbitration.

The Council followed the recommendation of the Court, to the effect that Terms of Reference should include "unless the Arbitral Tribunal considers it inappropriate, a list of issues to be determined." Article 18(d) of the Rules so provides. As noted previously, this maintains as the general rule that the Arbitral tribunal should attempt to set out, even if it be in summary and provisional fashion, a list of issues to be determined in the arbitration. It is left with the discretion, however, to eliminate such a list if it considers that it would be inappropriate.

The Council maintained, however, the blanket exclusion of liability clause which had been recommended by the Commission.[27]

Following the approval of the Rules which now incorporate a number of the former Internal Rules of the Court, and which include some new provisions concerning advances on costs, the Court and its Secretariat undertook the necessary revisions of the Court's Internal Rules (Appendix II to the Rules) and the Arbitration Costs and Fees (Appendix III to the Rules) to conform to the new Rules.[28] Modifications from the previous text are relatively minor and mostly self-explanatory, as shown in the annotated text to follow.[29] These modifications also enter into effect on January 1, 1998.

---

26 A well known Swiss lawyer from Geneva, and a former Chairman of a panel of the Iran U.S. Claims Tribunal, Dr. Briner succeeded to the post formerly occupied by Alain Plantay, a French national, on 1 January 1997. Dr. Briner attended the February meeting of the Commission and participated in discussions there.

27 *See* further discussion at commentary under Article 34.

28 The Statutes of the Court were also reorganized slightly, in conjunction with the modifications to the Internal Rules and the Arbitration Costs and Fees. The text of the 1998 Appendices to the Rules follows the annotated text at Appendix I, II and III, respectively.

29 One minor change of some interest is the removal of the restriction previously imposed (Internal Rules, 1988 ed. Article 3), on Vice Chairmen of the Court (of which there are presently eight) from acting as arbitrators or counsel in ICC

* * *

The overall impression of the new Rules, other than their unquestionably better organization and logical drafting, is one of substantial continuity. Specific measures have been taken to accelerate administrative handling of the file and to address problems which have arisen in the application of the 1975 Rules. In addition, arbitration procedures have been improved to correspond to the changing international environment by incorporating reforms which have been successfully adopted by other arbitration institutions. Two years of study by a very active Working Party of the ICC Arbitration Commission, reflections within the Court, and extensive consultations with the ICC's National Committees, and through them with ICC arbitration users, revealed substantial satisfaction with most of the traditional features of ICC arbitration. A consensus developed to support (sometimes with minor modifications) even practices which had been subject to certain criticisms in the past.[30]

A notable feature which has remained in the Rules, and has even been reinforced by the revision, is the discretionary powers of the Court. Consistent with the concept that the Rules should remain a short outline of the principles to be applied in the conduct and administration of the arbitration, the Court, as the body responsible for ensuring the application of the Rules,[31] has wide discretion to determine how the Rules should be applied in particular cases. A key illustration is Article 35, the General Rule, which provides, unchanged, that:

> "In all matters not expressly provided for in these Rules, the Court and the Arbitral Tribunal shall act in the spirit of these Rules and shall make every effort to make sure that the Award is enforceable at law."

The General Rule only reflects the principle that the Court has wide discretionary powers in administering the Rules. This has been accepted by the arbitration community and is reinforced by the provisions of the new Rules. For the Court's

---

arbitrations. This absolute restriction remains for the Chairman of the Court and members of the Secretariat. Members of the Court (and now its Vice Chairmen as well) may not be appointed by the Court as ICC arbitrators but they may so serve if nominated by a party or pursuant to a procedure agreed by the parties (Internal Rules, Article 2(2)).

30   This was the case, for example, with maintaining the necessity for the Court to make a prima facie determination that an arbitration agreement may exist as a condition to sending a matter to an arbitral tribunal for determination of the jurisdictional issue. *See* comment at Article 6(2), *infra.* Similarly the requirement of Terms of Reference was retained over some criticism to the effect that this requirement delays the arbitral process. A vast majority of the National Committee favored keeping the Terms, although there was some divergence, as noted above, as to their required contents.

31   Statutes, Article 1; Rules, Article 1.

most remarkable power — deciding on the challenge of an arbitrator — it is specifically provided that no reasons shall be given for its decision.[32] The Court is also not required to give reasons for other administrative decisions, and does not do so.[33] Amongst the discretionary powers of the Court may be mentioned: the Court's initial determination, to its *prima facie* satisfaction, that an arbitration agreement may exist, as a condition of the formation of an arbitral tribunal for the determination of jurisdictional (and other) issues (Article 6 (2)); determination of advances to be paid by the parties to cover ICC administrative costs and the fees and expenses of the arbitrators (Article 30 (2)); appointment, confirmation, challenge or replacement of an arbitrator (Article 7 (4)); determination (where the parties have not otherwise agreed) of whether the arbitral tribunal should be composed of one or three arbitrators (Article 8 (2)); determination where the parties have not agreed of the place of arbitration (Article 14 (1)); determination of an appropriate National Committee to propose an arbitrator (where the parties have not otherwise agreed) (Article 9 (3)); in multi-party arbitrations, where joint parties have not agreed to the joint nomination of an arbitrator, determination whether all arbitrators should be named by the Court, and if so, appointment of such arbitrators; determination whether to remove an arbitrator (Articles 12 (2)(3); where an arbitrator dies or is removed after the closing of proceedings, determination whether an arbitrator is to be replaced, or whether arbitral proceedings should continue before a "truncated tribunal" (Article 12 (5)); approval of the Terms of Reference (where the parties and arbitral tribunal have not agreed to the Terms) (Article 18 (3)); extension of time limits (Articles 24 (2), 32 (2)); and finally, at the end of arbitral proceedings, scrutiny of the Award (Article 27), and determination of the costs of the arbitration (Article 31).

A key to the Rules is thus the discretion given to the Court to make administrative decisions in a great variety of matters. This leads to a rather heavy administrative procedure: dossiers have to be prepared and staffed by the Secretariat to permit decisions either by the whole Court, sitting in plenary session (meeting, in principle, once a month) or three person Committees of the Court meeting more frequently and to which may be delegated powers by the Court.[34] A few new powers have been delegated to the Secretary General of the Court, as discussed earlier, in the interest of expediting the arbitral process; however a wider delegation of powers, though discussed, was not adopted. Essentially, consultations with the National Committees revealed a consensus that ICC

---

32 Rules, Article 7 (4) (essentially unchanged from the prior provision).

33 This is to be distinguished from informal, and sometimes very detailed, communications by the Secretariat which seek to keep the parties informed of all administrative measures affecting the proceedings.

34 Scrutiny of awards and decisions on the challenge or replacement of an arbitrator are functions traditionally reserved to the Court meeting in plenary session, although a modification in the Internal Rules no longer makes this a statutory requirement. *See* commentary on Internal Rule 4(5) at Article 11(3), Rules.

arbitration users were on the whole satisfied (at least in comparison with other alternatives) to leave discretionary administrative decision-making in the hands of the Court.

The revision of the Rules was accomplished by a lengthy consultative process involving the collaboration of the Court, the Commission on Arbitration, and the National Committees. The revision has clarified the Rules, adopted modifications in line with the developments in arbitration procedure, while at the same time keeping intact the traditional features of the ICC Rules.

Introduction to the Annotated Text

The text of the new ICC Arbitration Rules as approved by the ICC Council on April 8, 1997 in Shanghai and entering into effect on January 1, 1998, is set out below (in bold). It is followed by a section by section comparison with the text of the relevant section of the Rules previously in force, together with analysis, commentary, and relevant citations to other references.

The annotations are organized under the following headings:

Prior Text

Modification

Comment

Other References

PRIOR TEXT is the antecedent article or articles in the 1975 Rules of Arbitration, as amended and in force as of January 1, 1988, hereinafter referred to as the 1975 Rules, or of the 1980 Internal Rules, as amended and in force as of January 1, 1988, that correspond to the 1998 Article in question. The last full revision of the Rules dates from 1975 with relatively minor modifications having been made and incorporated therein as of January 1, 1988. The word NEW indicates that no corresponding subsection or article exists in the 1975 Rules.

MODIFICATION sets out the changes found in the new text, in general or specific terms depending upon the nature of the modification. If the modification is purely semantic, the exact change may not be cited.

COMMENT explains the motivation of the revision of an existing article or the incorporation of a new one, as well as the expected effect of such changes on ICC arbitration practice. If such change or new article incorporates or reflects ideas or wording from other established Arbitration Rules, the influence of such other rules may be noted. Arbitration Rules referred to include: the American Arbitration Association's International Arbitration Rules (the "AAA International Rules") as amended and effective on April 1, 1997; the American Arbitration Association's Commercial Arbitration Rules (the "AAA Commercial Rules") as amended and effective on November 1, 1993; the London Court of International Arbitration's Rules (the "LCIA Rules"), effective from January 1, 1985; the World Intellectual Property Organization Arbitration Rules (the "WIPO Rules") effective from October 1, 1994; the United Nations Commission on International Trade Law's Arbitration Rules (the "UNCITRAL Rules"), adopted on April 18, 1976; and the International Centre for Settlement of Investment Disputes Rules of Procedure for Arbitration Proceedings ("ICSID Arbitration Rules") effective from September 26, 1984.

OTHER REFERENCES lists the other sources from which the changes may have originated or comments on the subject matter of the article. In this section, COURT signifies the proposals for modification of the 1975 Rules made by the International Court of Arbitration (Doc. N° 420/338 of 14 March 1995).

References to other commentary and reports in publications and periodicals follow the abbreviations set out below.

Abbreviations

The following abbreviations are used:

C.P.&P.

> W. Laurence Craig, William W. Park, Jan Paulsson, International Chamber of Commerce Arbitration, Oceana/ICC Publishing, 2d. ed., 1990 (Third Edition scheduled for publication in 1998).

Dossiers of Institute

> ICC Institute of International Business Law and Practice, the Dossiers of the Institute.

IBA Ethics

> International Bar Association Ethics for International Arbitrators (1987).

ICC Bull.

> The ICC International Court of Arbitration Bulletin.

ICC Bull. Supp.

> November 1997 Special Supplement to *ICC Bull.* reporting the proceedings of the ICC conference on "The New 1998 ICC Rules of Arbitration".

1 ICC Collection

> S. Jarvin and Y. Derains, "Collection of ICC Arbitral Awards (Recueil des sentences arbitrales de la CCI) 1974-1985", Kluwer, 1990.

2 ICC Collection

> S. Jarvin, Y. Derains, J.J. Arnaldez, "Collection of ICC Arbitral Awards (Recueil des sentences arbitrales de la CCI) 1986-1990", Kluwer, 1994.

3 ICC Collection

> S. Jarvin, Y. Derains, J.J. Arnaldez, "Collection of ICC Arbitral Awards (Recueil des sentences arbitrales de la CCI) 1991-1995", Kluwer, 1997.

JDI

> Journal du Droit International (the last issue of each year of this quarterly contains extracts of ICC awards with commentary by Y. Derains, J.J. Arnaldez and D. Hascher).

J. Int'l Arb.

> Journal of International Arbitration.

Yearbook

> International Council for Commercial Arbitration (ICCA), Yearbook Commercial Arbitration (Kluwer).

ANNOTATED TEXT

INTRODUCTORY PROVISIONS

Article 1
International Court of Arbitration

1(1) The International Court of Arbitration (the "Court") of the International Chamber of Commerce (the "ICC") is the arbitration body attached to the ICC. The statutes of the Court are set forth in Appendix 1. Members of the Court are appointed by the Council of the ICC. The function of the Court is to provide for the settlement by arbitration of business disputes of an international character in accordance with the Rules of Arbitration of the International Chamber of Commerce (the "Rules"). If so empowered by an arbitration agreement, the Court shall also provide for the settlement by arbitration in accordance with these Rules of business disputes not of an international character.

PRIOR TEXT: Article 1 (1), 1975 Rules; Article 1, 1980 Internal Rules

Article 1(1) 1975 Rules

The International Court of Arbitration of the International Chamber of Commerce is the arbitration body attached to the International Chamber of Commerce. Members of the Court are appointed by the Council of the International Chamber of Commerce. The function of the Court is to provide for the settlement by arbitration of business disputes of an international character in accordance with these Rules.

Article 1 Internal Rules

The International Court of Arbitration may accept jurisdiction over business disputes not of an international business nature, if it has jurisdiction by reason of an arbitration agreement.

MODIFICATION: The "International Court of Arbitration", and the "International Chamber of Commerce" have been made defined terms thus permitting them to be referred to thereafter by the abbreviated titles of "the Court", and "the ICC". Article 1 refers to the source of the Court's powers (its "Statutes") and indicates that they can be found in Appendix 1. The last sentence regarding the Court's powers in business disputes not of an international nature incorporates Article 1 of the 1980 Internal Rules with slight editorial modification and with the further modification that the Court "shall", (not "may") provide for settlement by arbitration "in accordance with these Rules" of such business disputes when so empowered by an arbitration agreement.

COMMENT: The terms are given their abbreviated titles in this subsection so as to avoid the repetition of lengthy titles henceforth in the text. The addition to the Rules of the provision regarding disputes not of an international nature reflects policy to incorporate into the Rules provisions from the Internal Rules which are necessary or helpful to users. The text reflects the Court's practice as in the past it has shown a willingness to supervise without differentiation from the arbitration of international disputes, the arbitration of disputes not of an international nature.

The provision that the Court "shall" provide for settlement of such disputes responds to comments by some arbitration users, as expressed through National Committees, expressing reluctance to provide for ICC arbitration in agreements which might be considered as domestic, if there were any risk that the Court might exercise its discretion not to accept such a case. This modification eliminates the possibility that the domestic nature of a dispute will constitute a reason, in and of itself, for its non-acceptance by the Court.

In view of the liberal practice of the Court in the past, in proceeding with disputes not of an international character, little real change should be expected.

OTHER REFERENCES:

The Court recommended that the sentence "The Court may accept jurisdiction over any other business dispute if it has jurisdiction by reason of an arbitration agreement" be added to Article 1(1).

C. P. & P., Section 10.02: "Business disputes of an international character". This section describes the prior practice of the Court which, under the authority of Article 1 of the 1975 Rules, consistently supervised arbitration of disputes having any international connection whatsoever. Article 1 of the 1980 Internal Rules, gave the Court discretion to supervise the arbitration of domestic disputes, thus allowing it to accept any business dispute it considered appropriate without any obligation to weigh arguments concerning the international character of the dispute.

1(2) The Court does not itself settle disputes. It has the function of ensuring the application of these Rules. It draws up its own Internal Rules (Appendix II).

PRIOR TEXT: First sentence of Article 2(1), 1975 Rules; Article 1(2), 1975 Rules

Article 2(1)

The International Court of Arbitration does not itself settle disputes.

Article 1(2)

In principle, the Court meets once a month. It draws up its own internal regulations.

MODIFICATION: Terms previously defined are now abbreviated in the revised Rules. The phrase "It has the function of ensuring the application of these Rules" is taken directly from Article 3 "Functions and powers" of the Statutes of the Court, found in Appendix 1 to the prior Rules. The first sentence of Article 1(2), 1975 Rules has been omitted. The second sentence has been modified to now indicate where the Court's Internal Rules may be found.

COMMENT: One of the principles of the 1998 revision was to include in the Rules, and thus make prominently available to users, provisions of the Internal

Rules, the knowledge of which would be helpful or necessary for parties to ICC arbitrations.

1(3) The Chairman of the Court, or in the Chairman's absence or otherwise at his request, one of its Vice-Chairmen shall have the power to take urgent decisions on behalf of the Court, provided that any such decision is reported to the Court at its next session.

PRIOR TEXT: Article 1(3), 1975 Rules

Article 1(3)

The Chairman of the International Court of Arbitration or his deputy shall have power to take urgent decisions on behalf of the Court, provided that any such decision shall be reported to the Court at its next session.

MODIFICATION: "[H]is deputy" is replaced by "in the Chairman's absence or otherwise at his request one of its Vice-Chairmen,".

COMMENT: The Chairman does not have a deputy, but rather vice-chairmen who are authorized to act only in his absence or at his request. The revised article does not clearly specify which Vice-Chairman should be called upon to act in an urgent matter in the absence of the Chairman which suggests the possibility of "forum shopping" (that is, for a concerned party to seek out a Vice-Chairman known to it, or from its region of the world). No doubt this is a matter which will be worked out by internal instruction from the Chairman to his Vice-Chairmen and his designation of a specified Vice-Chairman to act in his absence.

OTHER REFERENCES:

C. P. & P., Section 2.03, "The Court". This section points out that in the past the power of the Chairman to take urgent decisions, which need only be reported to the Court at its next session and are not submitted for the Court's approval, has been theoretically broader than the powers of the three member Committee of the Court which pursuant to Article 11 of the 1980 Internal Rules was specifically not empowered to rule on challenges to arbitrators, determine that an arbitrator was not fulfilling his functions, or approve a draft award (except one made with the consent of the parties). Article 4(5) of the 1998 Internal Rules simply specifies that the Court shall determine the decisions which may be taken by the Committee. For current powers delegated to the Committee, *see* Comment under Article 1(4) of the Arbitration Rules and p. 192, *infra*.

The Chairman's power to take urgent decisions on an expedited basis is the key to successful implementation of "fast-track" arbitration by the ICC when the parties have agreed to shortened procedural deadlines. In a matter where two related complex arbitrations were resolved within two months of the initial Request, the Chairman took decisions on such matters as: determination of the *prima facie* existence of the arbitration agreement, constitution of the arbitral tribunal, choice of the place of arbitration, fixing of the advances on costs, ruling on objections to the appointment of an arbitrator, approval of the draft award and fixing of arbitrators' fees and administrative expenses. *See* Memorandum from the ICC Secretariat on Fast-Track Arbitration, 2 *Am. Rev. Int'l Arb.* 162 (1991), B. Davis, Fast-Track Arbitration: Different Perspectives. The case viewed by a Counsel at the ICC Court's Secretariat, 3 *ICC Bull., N°2,4* (1992).

See Article 2(2), 1998 Internal Rules. A Vice-Chairman may be called upon, from time to time, to take over any of the functions of the Chairman. Accordingly, under the prior Internal Rules, a Vice-Chairman was subject to the same disabilities as the Chairman including the prohibition from acting as an arbitrator in ICC arbitrations. Over the last few years a practice has developed to appoint more Vice-Chairman (there are now eight) with the apparent intent of broadening participation geographically and otherwise, and with the result that it is less likely that any particular Vice-Chairman would be called upon to serve in the place of the Chairman. In these circumstances, the position of a Vice-Chairman may be closer to that of ordinary members than that of the Chairman, and the additional disability may not be required. Article 2(2) of the 1998 Internal Rules [Appendix II], maintains the prohibition for the Chairman and members of the Secretariat to act as arbitrators in ICC arbitrations. The prohibition no longer applies to Vice-Chairmen who may be proposed as an arbitrator by a party or by any other procedure agreed by the parties for confirmation by the Court. They cannot be directly appointed by the Court.

See 8 Yearbook 204 (1983) for the report of an urgent decision by the Chairman determining *prima facie* the existence of an arbitration agreement covering the parent company of a group and ordering that the arbitration proceed (with comment of Sigvard Jarvin, former general counsel of the Court).

See "ICC Fast-Track Arbitration: Different Perspectives", 3 *ICC Bull.* N°2, 4 (1992); *See also,* "Special Section: Fast-Track Arbitration", 2 *Am. Rev. Int'l Arb.* 138 (1991).

1(4) As provided for in its Internal Rules, the Court may delegate to one or more committees composed of its members the power to take certain decisions, provided that any such decision is reported to the Court at its next session.

PRIOR TEXT: Article 1(4), 1975 Rules

Article 1(4)

The Court may, in the manner provided for in its internal regulations, delegate to one or more groups of its members the power to take certain decisions provided that any such decision shall be reported to the Court at its next session.

MODIFICATION: "Internal Regulations" becomes "Internal Rules" with a reference to Appendix II. The subparagraph has been reorganized and rewritten for clarity.

COMMENT: The ability of the Court to delegate decision making on many questions to a three member "Committees of the Court" has been essential to permit it to deal with the increasing number of cases being submitted to ICC arbitration. Three member committees (of varying composition) meet twice a month (in addition to the Court's monthly plenary session). Decision making power can be delegated to the Committees on all issues other than challenges to or removal of arbitrators and approval of awards.

OTHER REFERENCES:

C. P.& P., Section 2.03, "The Court".

The Court's delegation of powers to a three man Committee of the Court, and the conditions for exercise of such powers, are set out in Article 4 of the 1998 Internal Rules, (Appendix II) which provides:

> 4(1) In accordance with the provisions of Article 1(4) of the Rules and Article 5 of its Statutes (Appendix I), the Court hereby establishes a Committee of the Court.

> 4(2) The members of the Committee consist of a Chairman and at least two other members. The Chairman of the Court acts as the Chairman of the Committee. If absent, the Chairman may designate a Vice-Chairman of the Court, or in exceptional circumstances, another member of the Court as Chairman of the Committee.

> 4(3) The other two members of the Committee are appointed by the Court from among the Vice-Chairmen or the other members of the Court. At each Plenary Session the Court appoints the members who are to attend the meetings of the Committee to be held before the next Plenary Session.

> 4(4) The Committee meets when convened by its Chairman. Two members constitute a quorum.

> 4(5) a) The Court shall determine the decisions that may be taken by the Committee.

> b) The decisions of the Committee are taken unanimously.

> c) When the Committee cannot reach a decision or deems it preferable to abstain, it transfers the case to the next Plenary Session, making any suggestions it deems appropriate.

> d) The Committee's decisions are brought to the notice of the Court at its next Plenary Session.

The Court has announced that under the 1998 Rules the Committee will be empowered to approve draft awards in some matters but that it will remain without power to rule on challenges to arbitrators or to determine that an arbitrator is not fufilling his functions. *See* Comment on p. 192, *infra*.

1(5) The Secretariat of the Court (the "Secretariat") under the direction of its Secretary General (the "Secretary General") shall have its seat at the headquarters of the ICC.

PRIOR TEXT:

Article 1(5), 1975 Rules.

Article 1(5)

The Secretariat of the International Court of Arbitration shall be at the Headquarters of the International Chamber of Commerce.

MODIFICATION: "under the direction of its Secretary General" is appended to the description of the Secretariat. The Secretariat is described as having its "seat" at the headquarters of the ICC.

COMMENT: Revisions in the 1998 Rules delegate certain administrative powers to the Secretary General in the interest of reducing delays (*see* Articles 9(2), 30 (1)). For this reason it was thought desirable to refer directly in the Rules to the office of Secretary General, and the Secretary General's relationship to the Secretariat. Other provisions concerning the Secretary General are found in the 1998 Internal Rules (Article 1(4), 1(5), 2(3), 3(2)).

The term "seat" is used in the sense of the legal domicile or official place of business of the Secretariat. The headquarters of the ICC, which was established, under the French law of 1901, as a non-profit membership association representing a confederation of national committees with the purpose of promoting world commerce, are in Paris. One of the reasons for providing explicitly that the legal domicile and official place of business of the Secretariat is at ICC headquarters in Paris is that for the first time the ICC Secretariat will have an overseas extension, having established in 1997 an administrative office in Hong Kong.

OTHER REFERENCES:

C.P. &P., Section 2.04, "The Secretariat".

Article 2
Definitions

In these Rules:

i) "Arbitral Tribunal" includes one or more arbitrators.

ii) "Claimant" includes one or more claimants and "Respondent" includes one or more respondents.

iii) "Award" includes, *inter alia*, **an interim, partial or final Award.**

PRIOR TEXT: i. Article 2(2), 1975 Rules

Article 2(2)

. . . In the following Articles the word "arbitrator" denotes a single arbitrator or three arbitrators as the case might be.

> ii. NEW

> iii. NEW

MODIFICATION: The article itself, entitled "Definitions", is new. The second sentence of Article 2(2), 1975 Rules is revised and included as Section i). The new Rules use the term "Arbitral Tribunal" throughout, instead of "arbitrator" which was used in the 1975 Rules. Section ii), and Section iii) are new.

COMMENT: The modifications reflect policy to define terms as early in the text of the Rules as possible to avoid later repetition. The definition of "Claimant" and "Respondent" to include the plural as well as the singular facilitates drafting in subsequent articles and is required in particular for the article on multi-party arbitration (*see* Article 10). The definition of the term "Award" is necessary to insure that any decision of an Arbitral Tribunal in the form of an award is subject to the scrutiny of the Court under Article 27 and the other formalities concerning awards. Interim and partial awards are final as to the matters which they decide although not final in the sense that they are not the last award the Arbitral Tribunal will make in the dispute. The definition of "award" manifests the desire to eliminate any lacuna in the text of the 1998 Rules.

OTHER REFERENCES:

The WIPO Rules contain a section of definitions at Article 1, entitled "Abbreviated Expressions":

> In these Rules:

> Arbitration Agreement" means an agreement by the parties to submit to arbitration all or certain disputes which have arisen or which may arise between them; an Arbitration Agreement may be in the form of an arbitration clause in a contract or in the form of a separate contract;

"Claimant" means the party initiating an arbitration;

"Respondent" means the party against which the arbitration is initiated, as named in the Request for Arbitration;

"WIPO" means the World Intellectual Property Organization;

"Center" means the WIPO Arbitration Center, a unit of the International Bureau of WIPO;

Words used in the singular include the plural and vice versa, as the context may require.

For discussion of the term "interim", "partial" and "final" award, *see* "Report of the Working Party of the ICC's Commission on International Arbitration on Dissenting Opinions and Interim and Partial Awards Vol. 1"; *ICC Bull.* No. 2 (1990), reprinted in II C.P. &P., Appendix V, (Loose leaf edition).

Article 3
Written Notifications or Communications; Time Limits

3(1) All pleadings and other written communications submitted by any party, as well as all documents annexed thereto, shall be supplied in a number of copies sufficient to provide one copy for each party, plus one for each arbitrator, and one for the Secretariat. A copy of any communication from the Arbitral Tribunal to the parties shall be sent to the Secretariat.

PRIOR TEXT: Article 6(1); NEW

Article 6(1)

All pleadings and written statements submitted by the parties, as well as all documents annexed thereto, shall be supplied in a number of copies sufficient to provide one copy for each party, plus one for each arbitrator, and one for the Secretariat.

MODIFICATION: The first sentence now refers to all pleadings and "other" written communications, and "any party" rather than "the parties". The second sentence of Article 3(1) has been added.

COMMENT: The first sentence has been modified for purposes of clarity. The second sentence has been added to indicate that arbitrators are required to communicate a copy to the Secretariat of any communication they may send to the parties. This confirms current recommended practices. Communications among the arbitrators are ordinarily not communicated to the Secretariat. While this Article prescribes the number of copies of pleadings, written communications, and annexed documents that a party shall submit, it does not state to whom. Articles 4 and 5 provide that for Requests, Answers and Counterclaims all copies will be submitted to the Secretariat who will communicate the requisite copies to the other party and the Arbitral Tribunal. In accordance with past practice, subsequent pleadings and written communications may be sent directly to the other party and the arbitrators with a copy to the Secretariat.

OTHER REFERENCES:

New Articles 1(6) and 1(7) of the 1998 Internal Rules define the custodianship obligations of the Secretariat concerning the documents received.

> 1(6) The Secretariat will in each case submitted to arbitration under the Rules retain in the archives of the Court all awards, terms of reference, and decisions of the Court as well as copies of the pertinent correspondence of the Secretariat.

> 1(7) Any documents, communications or correspondence submitted by the parties or the arbitrators may be destroyed unless a party or an arbitrator requests in writing within a period fixed by the Secretariat the return of such documents. All related costs and expenses for the return of those documents shall be paid by such party or arbitrator.

These new internal rules reflects current practice. With the growth of ICC arbitration, both in number and size and complexity, and the requirement that all pleadings, a copy of memorials, documents and exhibits be filed with the Secretariat, the ICC has become overburdened with massive storage requirements. These provisions of the Internal Rules permit the ICC, as supervisor and administrator of arbitration, to retain the essential documentation to be able to assist parties with enforcement of awards and administrative follow-up without accepting an open-ended obligation as custodian of historical files.

3(2) All notifications or communications from the Secretariat and the Arbitral Tribunal shall be made to the last address of the party or its representative for whom the same are intended, as notified either by the party in question or by the other party.   Such notification or communication may be made by delivery against receipt, registered post, courier, facsimile transmission, telex, telegram or any other means of telecommunication that provides a record of the sending thereof.

PRIOR TEXT: Article 6(2), 1975 Rules

Article 6(2)

All notifications or communications from the Secretariat and the arbitrator shall be validly made if they are delivered against receipt or forwarded by registered post to the address or last known address of the party for whom the same are intended as notified by the party in question or by the other party as appropriate.

MODIFICATION: The modified article permits notification from the Secretariat and the Arbitral Tribunal to the parties by more modern types of communication than registered mail, including electronic means of communication, as long as such means "provide a record of the sending thereof". The subsection is reorganized slightly.

COMMENT: The modification is designed to permit notification by modern means of telecommunication, as well as traditional means, without stipulating what means are permissible provided a record of the sending of the communication is established. The practice of the Secretariat, to use all possible means to ensure that communications are actually received, will not be changed. The presumption of receipt by the party of a document mailed by registered mail to the indicated address is extended to other means of communication which establish sending to that address. These modifications provide for the use of modern communication technology while continuing to emphasize the necessity of establishing a record of the sending of the communication.

Note that this direction applies only to notification and communication by the Secretariat and by the Arbitral Tribunal. It does not apply by its terms to communications from and between the parties (although it may be a useful guideline for them). Frequently the agreed means for such communications will be set out in the Terms of Reference.

Delivery against receipt is one of the methods of communication set out in Article 3(2) but the Rules require only the proof of the sending of the communication by the prescribed means, and where proof of such sending is established the document shall, pursuant to Article 3(3), be deemed to have been received.

The provision that a notification or communication made to a party to the last address communicated by that party or to the address communicated "by the other party" does not guarantee that the notification or communication will in fact be received. Although both the Secretariat and the Arbitral Tribunal will take every reasonable precaution, where there are reasons to doubt the validity or the continued validity of the address, to assure that a document is effectively received by the party, any notification or communication which satisfies the conditions of Article 3(2) complies with the Rules and permits the arbitration to proceed.

Omission of the word "validly" from the prior Article's provision that "All notifications or communications from the Secretariat and the arbitrators shall be validly made" is not intended to affect the efficacity of notification and communication made according to the Rules. The omission reflects the understanding that the validity of a communication for the purpose of determining the validity and effect of the award is ultimately determined under national law. *See* Comment under Article 3(3).

OTHER REFERENCES:

C.P. & P., Section 10.07, "Notifications and Communications and Calculation of Periods of Time".

The Court: The Court recommended the addition of "Such notifications or communications may also be made by any means of telecommunication that provides a record thereof, the original document governing in the event of any dispute", to Article 3(2).

The WIPO Rules provide in Article 4 "Notices, Periods of Time": " (a) Any notice or other communication that may or is required to be given under these Rules shall be in writing and shall be delivered by expedited postal or courier service, or transmitted by telex, telefax or other means of telecommunication that provide a record thereof. (b) A party's last known residence or place of business shall be a valid address for the purpose of any notice or other communication in the absence of any notification of a change by that party. Communications may in any event be addressed to a party in the manner stipulated, or failing such a stipulation, according to the practice followed in the course of dealing between the parties".

3(3) A notification or communication shall be deemed to have been made on the day it was received by the party itself or by its representative, or would have been received if made in accordance with the preceding paragraph.

PRIOR TEXT: Article 6(3), 1975 Rules

Article 6(3)

Notification or communication shall be deemed to have been effected on the day when it was received, or should, if made in accordance with the preceding paragraph, have been received by the party itself or by its representative.

MODIFICATION: Substitution of "would" for "should" is a grammatical correction. The subsection has been reorganized for clarity.

COMMENT: Subsections (1) and (2) of Article 3 inform the Arbitrators and the Secretariat as to how notification and communication shall be made in order to comply with the Rules. If communications or notices are made in this way they will be deemed to have been received and arbitration proceedings cannot be prevented from proceeding based simply on a party's claim of non-receipt. Both the Secretariat and Arbitral Tribunal take every measure possible to ensure actual receipt. The international environment can in some instances make it difficult to prove actual receipt and may facilitate a defaulting party's bad faith attempt to avoid acknowledgment of receipt which is a reason for the present text.

By agreeing to the Rules under which the arbitration shall be governed, a party is deemed to have accepted that notices and communications, if made as prescribed by the Rules, shall be presumed to have been received. However, the definitive validity of an arbitration award, if a party were to argue that it was unable to present its claim or make its defense because of non-receipt of important communications or notifications, would ultimately be determined by the courts of any state where the award was put in issue by judicial recourse or recognition and enforcement proceedings.

OTHER REFERENCES:

C.P. & P., Section 10.07, "Notifications, Communications and Calculation of Time".

3(4) Periods of time specified in, or fixed under the present Rules, shall start to run on the day following the date a notification or communication is deemed to have been made in accordance with the preceding paragraph. When the day next following such date is an official holiday, or a non-business day in the country where the notification or communication is deemed to have been made, the period of time shall commence on the first following business day. Official holidays and non-business days are included in the calculation of the period of time. If the last day of the relevant period of time granted is an official holiday or a non-business day in the country where the notification or communication is deemed to have been made, the period of time shall expire at the end of the first following business day.

PRIOR TEXT: Article 6(4), 1975 Rules

Article 6(4)

Periods of time specified in the present Rules or in the Internal Rules or set by the International Court of Arbitration pursuant to its authority under any of these Rules shall start to run on the day following the date a notification or communication is deemed to have been effected in accordance with the preceding paragraph. When, in the country where the notification or communication is deemed to have been effected, the day next following such date is an official holiday or a non-business day, the period of time shall commence on the first following working day. Official holidays and non-working days are included in the calculation of the period of time. If the last day of the relevant period of time granted is an official holiday or a non-business day in the country where the notification or communication is deemed to have been effected, the period of time shall expire at the end of the first following working day.

MODIFICATION: The term "business day(s)" is used in place of "working day(s)". The first sentence has been simplified to read "periods of time specified in or fixed under the present rules shall start to run. . . ". Some minor modifications have been made in the interests of clarity.

COMMENT: References to "working day" have been changed to "business day" to remain consistent with the term used throughout the Rules. The Article provides for the calculation of time for periods not only "specified in" but also "fixed under" under the Rules, hence applying to time periods that may be set by the Arbitral Tribunal, the Court or the Secretariat. Such specification creates an "umbrella term" therefore permitting the other conditions under which periods of time could be set to be omitted from the first sentence of the new article.

OTHER REFERENCES:

C.P. & P., Section 10.07, "Notifications, Communication and Calculation of Time".

WIPO Rules, Article 4(e):

> (e) For the purpose of calculating a period of time under these Rules, such period shall begin to run on the day following the day when a notice or other communication is received. If the last day of such period is an official holiday or a non-business day at the residence or place of business of the addressee, the period is extended until the first business day which follows. Official holidays or non-business days occurring during the running of the period of time are included in calculating the period.

UNCITRAL Rules, Article 2(2):

> 2. For the purposes of calculating a period of time under these Rules, such period shall begin to run on the day following the day when a notice, notification, communication or proposal is received. If the last day of such period is an official holiday or a non-business day at the residence or place of business of the addressee, the period is extended until the first business day which follows. Official holidays or non-business days occurring during the running of the period of time are included in calculating the period.

COMMENCING THE ARBITRATION

Article 4
Request for Arbitration

4(1) A party wishing to have recourse to arbitration under these Rules shall submit its Request for Arbitration (the "Request") to the Secretariat, which shall notify the Claimant and Respondent of the receipt of the Request and the date of such receipt.

PRIOR TEXT: First two sentences of Article 3(1), 1975 Rules, substantially modified.

Article 3(1)

A party wishing to have recourse to arbitration by the International Chamber of Commerce shall submit its Request for Arbitration to the Secretariat of the International Court of Arbitration, through its National Committee or directly. In this latter case the Secretariat shall bring the Request to the notice of the National Committee concerned.

MODIFICATION: The phrase "under these Rules" replaces "by the International Chamber of Commerce". The defining term (the "Request") is appended to the term "Request for Arbitration". The section of subparagraph 1 of Article 3(1) of the 1975 Rules, providing the option of submitting a request for arbitration through a National Committee, is eliminated.

COMMENT: The minor changes in wording, and the addition of defined terms, reflect the drafters' intention to simplify and make uniform the text of the Rules. The omitted provision which allowed submission of the Request through National Committees was very seldom used in practice. The option was a source of confusion and detracted from the prescribed confidentiality of the arbitral proceedings, as well as causing unnecessary transmittal expenses for the National Committees themselves. The concluding phrase of subparagraph 1 has been added to specify clearly the duties of the Secretariat upon receipt of a Request.

The provision in Article 4(1) that the Secretariat shall notify both Claimant and Respondent of the date of receipt of a Request should be contrasted with the provision of Article 4(5) that the Secretariat shall forward the Request and documents only after having received the required advance payment and the necessary number of copies. In other words, the Respondent will be notified of the pendency of a Request immediately, but will learn of its contents only after the Claimant has fulfilled the required conditions. The purpose is to avoid a "limping" situation, unfair to the Respondent, where a Request has been filed but the Respondent is not made aware that it is the subject of proceedings because administrative requirements have not been fulfilled.

OTHER REFERENCES:

C.P. & P., Section 10.04, "The Request for Arbitration".

4(2) The date on which the Request is received by the Secretariat shall, for all purposes, be deemed to be the date of the commencement of the arbitral proceedings.

PRIOR TEXT: Third sentence of Article 3(1), 1975 Rules

Article 3(1)

The date when the Request is received by the Secretariat of the Court shall, for all purposes, be deemed to be the date of commencement of the arbitral proceedings.

MODIFICATION: "[O]n which" replaces "when".

COMMENT: This provision makes clear that even if the Request is served upon the Respondent, prior to being received by the Secretariat, the official date of the Request is still that of its receipt by the Secretariat.

OTHER REFERENCES:

C.P. & P., Section 10.04, "The Request for Arbitration".

4(3) The Request shall, *inter alia,* contain the following information:

a) the name in full, description and address of each of the parties;

b) a description of the nature and circumstances of the dispute giving rise to the claims;

c) a statement of the relief sought including, to the extent possible, an indication of any amount(s) claimed;

d) the relevant agreements and, in particular, the arbitration agreement;

e) all relevant particulars concerning the number of arbitrators and their choice in accordance with the provisions of Articles 8, 9 and 10, and any nomination of an arbitrator required thereby; and

f) any comments as to the place of arbitration, the applicable rules of law and the language of the arbitration.

PRIOR TEXT: Article 3(2) of 1975 Rules.

Article 3(2)

The Request for Arbitration shall inter alia contain the following information:

a) names in full, description, and addresses of the parties,

b) a statement of the Claimant's case,

c) the relevant agreements, and in particular the agreement to arbitrate, and such documentation or information as will serve clearly to establish the circumstances of the case,

d) all relevant particulars concerning the number of arbitrators and their choice in accordance with the provisions of Article 2 above.

MODIFICATION: The heading of Subsection 4(3) and the provision of Subsection 4(3) (a) are left, for the most part, unchanged. Subsection 4(3) (b) is changed from "a statement of the claimant's case," to "a description of the nature and circumstances of the dispute". Subsection 4(3) (c) is new and introduces a supplementary requirement of information: "Statement of the relief sought including to the extent possible an indication of any amounts claimed". In subsection 4(3) (d) [3(2) (c) of the 1975 Rules] "agreement to arbitrate" is replaced by "arbitration agreement" and the requirement to supply additional documentation or information is eliminated. Subsection 4(3) (e) [3(2) (d) of the 1975 Rules] is left unchanged with the exception of the replacement of reference to Article 2 with reference to Article 8, 9 and 10 to comply with the most recent organization of the Rules.   Subsection 4(3) (f) is new, establishing that the Request for Arbitration must now include: "any comments as to the place of arbitration, the applicable rules of law and the language of the arbitration". .

COMMENT: With respect to subsection 4(3) (b) the drafters of the revised Rules considered the requirement previously set out at Article 3(2) (b) that the Request for Arbitration contain a "statement of the Claimant's case" unnecessarily burdensome at so early a stage of the proceedings; moreover, it was considered that the Claimant's case could be developed in the subsequent written pleadings that would be authorized by the Arbitral Tribunal. Some confusion has been observed in the past due to the sentiment of civil law lawyers that a "statement of case" must require a detailed reference to what was expected to be proved and the evidence therefor while common law lawyers understood it to mean simply the pleading of issues sufficient to give notice of the elements of the claim with sufficient allegations of fact to make out a claim at law ("notice pleading").

For the same reason, it is no longer required that there be appended to the Request "such documentation or information as will serve clearly to establish the circumstances of the case". On the other hand the requirement of Article 4(3) (d) that the Request contain "the relevant agreements and in particular the arbitration agreement" implies that at least some basic documents should be supplied.

The reduction of formal requirements for a Request for Arbitration may also be a reaction to dilatory tactics whereby defendants occasionally alleged that they were not required to file an Answer (thus delaying the preparation of the Terms of Reference and the arbitral proceedings) because the Request did not comply with the Rules. While the formal requirements for the Request have thus been relaxed, the change does not imply that arbitral proceedings can be commenced by giving notice of an intent to arbitrate to be followed subsequently by making a claim. This is the two step procedure provided under the UNCITRAL Rules where a party can simply commence an arbitration by notification of the existence of a dispute and then submit its claim by means of a Statement of Claim to be filed within the time period provided by the Arbitral Tribunal (UNCITRAL Rules, Article 18). The combined effect of Articles 4(3) (b) and (c) of the 1998 Rules is still that the claimant should provide a description of the dispute, its claim, and the relief sought. Whether or not this is considered a "statement of Claimant's case" may be more a question of terminology than anything else.

The added requirement at Article 4(3) (c) that the Claimant set out, to the extent possible, "an indication of any amounts claimed" is useful to the Court in determining (when it must make this choice) whether a sole arbitrator or a tribunal of three arbitrators should be constituted, and the amount of the advances on costs (*see* Article 30).

The introduction of Article 4(3) (f) should assist the Court in its appointment or confirmation of arbitrators (Article 9) and its fixing or confirmation of the place of arbitration (Article 14(1)). The views of the parties as to the language of the arbitration are relevant to the Court's selection of arbitrators. If disputed, the language (or languages) of the arbitration is an issue to be determined by the Arbitral Tribunal. The information required in Article 4(3) (f) is also useful to the arbitrators in drawing up the Terms of Reference.

OTHER REFERENCES:

C.P.&P., Section 10.04, "The Request for Arbitration", describes prior practice and counsels the filing of sufficient details in the Request, and documents relied on, to permit the Defendant to file a responsive pleading and to facilitate the tasks of the Court (in constituting the Tribunal) and the Arbitral Tribunal (in drawing up the Terms of Reference). Quite apart from facilitating these procedural steps, the Claimant who files a clear statement of its claim and its position on the dispute between the parties will create a positive first impression with the Arbitral Tribunal.

See Working Party on the Revision of the ICC Rules of Arbitration, Doc. N° 420/344 (December 28, 1995).

See UNCITRAL Arbitration Rules, Article 3(3).

See ICC Arbitration N° 6784 of 1990, 8. *ICC Bull.* N° 1, 53 (Request for arbitration filed by fax and without copy of arbitration agreement sufficient to constitute a request for arbitration and validly initiate proceedings).

4(4) Together with the Request, the Claimant shall submit the number of copies thereof required by Article 3(1) and shall make the advance payment on administrative expenses required by Appendix III ("Arbitration Costs and Fees") in force on the date the Request is submitted. In the event that the Claimant fails to comply with either of these requirements, the Secretariat may fix a time limit within which the Claimant must comply, failing which the file shall be closed without prejudice to the right of the Claimant to submit the same claims at a later date in another Request.

PRIOR TEXT: NEW

MODIFICATION: N.A.

COMMENT: This new provision sets out clearly the conditions which must be fulfilled by the Claimant prior to the setting in motion of the arbitration timetable by the Secretariat's transmission of the Request to the Respondent. The initial advance payment is simply a filing fee (presently $ 2,500). If the Claimant does not fulfill the conditions within the time limit set by the Secretariat, the file may be closed. The closing of the file by the Secretariat is without prejudice to the later resubmission of the claim, accompanied by the required documents and advance payments. Note that any such resubmission must be by "another Request"; the Request would thus be considered a new one for statute of limitations and other purposes.

OTHER REFERENCES:

C.P.&P., Section 21.02, "ICC Administrative Costs".

The LCIA Rules provide at Article 1:

> Any party wishing to commence an arbitration under these Rules ('the Claimant') shall send to the Registrar of the Court ('the Registrar') a written request for arbitration ('the Request') which shall include, or be accompanied by:
>
> . . .
>
> (f) the fee prescribed in the Schedule of Costs.

4(5) The Secretariat shall send a copy of the Request and the documents annexed thereto to the Respondent for its Answer to the Request once the Secretariat has sufficient copies of the Request and the required advance payment.

PRIOR TEXT: Article 3(3).

Article 3(3)

The Secretariat shall send a copy of the Request and the documents annexed thereto to the Defendant for his Answer.

MODIFICATION: "Respondent" is used in place of "defendant" throughout the Rules. (*See* definition of "Respondent" in Article 2(ii)). The provisional clause "once the Secretariat has sufficient copies of the Request and the required advance payment" is added to the first sentence.

COMMENT: Where the conditions for forwarding the Request to the Respondent have not been complied with the Respondent will nevertheless be informed that a Request has been filed. (*See* Article 4(1) *supra*). The closing of the file by the Secretariat is without prejudice to the future filing of a Request that fulfills the requirements of the Rules. (*See* Article 4(4), *supra*).

OTHER REFERENCES:

4(6) When a party submits a Request in connection with a legal relationship in respect of which arbitration proceedings between the same parties are already pending under these Rules, the Court may, at the request of a party, decide to include the claims contained in the Request in the pending proceedings provided that the Terms of Reference have not been signed or approved by the Court. Once the Terms of Reference have been signed or approved by the Court, claims may only be included in the pending proceedings subject to the provisions of Article 19.

PRIOR TEXT: Article 13, 1980 Internal Rules

Article 13

When a party presents a Request for Arbitration in connection with a legal relationship already submitted to arbitration proceedings by the same parties and pending before the International Court of Arbitration, the Court may decide to include that claim in the existing proceedings, subject to the provisions of Article 16 of the ICC Rules of Arbitration.

MODIFICATIONS: The provision allowing claims "in connection with a legal relationship in respect of which arbitration proceedings between the same parties are already pending" to be joined to a Request for Arbitration already in action, is carried over, and now expressly provides that such joinder must be "at the request of a party". The new subsection also states that such joinder can only occur "provided that the Terms of Reference have not been signed or approved by the Court". If the Terms of Reference in the pending proceedings have already been so signed or approved, consolidation of the claims can take place only with the agreement of the Arbitral Tribunal (Article 19).

COMMENT: This article permits consolidation of disputes calling for ICC arbitration between the same parties, usually under separate contracts, in a single arbitral proceeding. Usually this is accomplished only with the agreement of both parties, as a party which does not wish consolidation may insist, in the case of a three person Arbitral Tribunal, on nominating a different arbitrator for the different contractual disputes, a situation which the Court has not resisted very strenuously in past practice although it has the power to do so under this provision and its predecessor.

Consolidation of arbitration proceedings between the same parties presents some of the same problems in respect to the constitution of a tribunal of three arbitrators as are encountered in multi-party arbitrations (*see* Article 10). A party who does not wish the two disputes to be heard together may insist on his right to nominate a different arbitrator under each of the applicable arbitration clauses. Deprivation of this "right" due to consolidation does not raise the same problem of lack of equality between the parties as in multi-party arbitration where each of the multiple parties risk losing any right to nominate an arbitrator at all, while the opposing party is free to nominate its arbitrator (except as otherwise provided under Article 10). The Court must balance the interest of one party in having disputes under separate contracts and separate arbitration clauses arbitrated separately with the interest of economy and arbitral efficiency, as urged by the other party, in having intertwined disputes heard together where both parties have agreed to ICC arbitration of the disputes. These issues arise even where the arbitration clauses provide, or the Court has found, that arbitration should proceed before a sole arbitrator.

Parties should be aware of the possibility in some jurisdictions (*e.g.*, the Netherlands) to obtain court ordered consolidation.

OTHER REFERENCES:

See P. Leboulanger, "Multi-Contract Arbitration", 13 *J. Int. Arb.* No. 4, p. 43 (1996) (a detailed description of ICC arbitration consolidation practice criticizing the Court for not taking a more robust position on consolidating arbitrations between the same parties even though one party will not consent).

See P. Level, "Joinder of Proceedings, Intervention of third parties, and additional claims and counterclaims", 7 *ICC Bull.* No. 2, p. 36, 44 (1996).

For a complex case where the French courts set aside an ICC award finding liability of certain Respondents based on obligations arising from a combination of duties under separate contracts whose consolidation had been ordered by the ICC Court, *see* OIAETI et Sofidif v. Cogema, Seru, Eurodif, CEA, Cour d'Appel de Versailles, 7 March 1990, 1991 *Rev. arb.* 326, Note E. Loquin (issues of multi-party arbitration also involved).

Article 5
Answer to the Request; Counterclaims

5(1) Within 30 days from the receipt of the Request from the Secretariat, the Respondent shall file an Answer (the "Answer") which shall, *inter alia*, contain the following information:

a) its name in full, description and address;

b) its comments as to the nature and circumstances of the dispute giving rise to the claim(s);

c) its response to the relief sought;

d) any comments concerning the number of arbitrators and their choice in light of the Claimant's proposals and in accordance with the provisions of Articles 8, 9 and 10, and any nomination of an arbitrator required thereby; and

e) any comments as to the place of arbitration, the applicable rules of law and the language of the arbitration.

PRIOR TEXT: First two sentences of Article 4(1), 1975 Rules.

Article 4(1)

The Defendant shall within 30 days from the receipt of the documents referred to in paragraph 3 of Article 3 comment on the proposals made concerning the number of arbitrators and their choice and, where appropriate, nominate an arbitrator. He shall at the same time set out his defense and supply relevant documents.

MODIFICATION: First sentence now includes clarification ". . . 30 days from the receipt of the Request from the Secretariat". Article 5(1) is reorganized with sub-headings conforming the requirements for the Answer to the organization of Article 4(3) ("Request for Arbitration"). The term "Answer" is assigned an abbreviation.

COMMENT: The parties are, with the revision of the first sentence, made aware that the time limit within which the Respondent must file its Answer begins to run upon receipt of the Request from the Secretariat. This modification will ensure that parties do not consider the time limit to have begun any time before the notification of the Request by the Secretariat. The format of this subsection as well as any additions or modifications to same have been made to conform with Article 4(3), "Request for Arbitration" and the comments thereunder are applicable.

OTHER REFERENCES:

C.P.&P., Section 10.05, "Answer and Counterclaim".

5(2) The Secretariat may grant the Respondent an extension of the time for filing the Answer, provided the application for such an extension contains the Respondent's comments concerning the number of arbitrators and their choice, and, where required by Articles 8, 9 and 10, the nomination of an arbitrator. If the Respondent fails to do so, the Court shall proceed in accordance with these Rules.

PRIOR TEXT: Final three sentences of Article 4(1) of 1975 Rules:

In exceptional circumstances the Defendant may apply to the Secretariat for an extension of time for the filing of his defense and his documents. The application must, however, include the Defendant's comments on the proposals made with regard to the number of arbitrators and their choice and also, where appropriate, the nomination of an arbitrator. If the Defendant fails to do so, the Secretariat shall report to the International Court of Arbitration, which shall proceed with the arbitration in accordance with these Rules.

MODIFICATION: The requirement provided in Article 4(1) of the 1975 Rules that an extension of time may be granted only "in exceptional circumstances" has been eliminated. Reference to Articles 8, 9 and 10 has been added.

COMMENT: It was recognized that in many circumstances it is not appropriate to require an Answer on the merits within 30 days. Prior practice reveals that extensions to answer the Request for Arbitration are frequently granted by the Court and that justifying circumstances are not "exceptional". Even if granted an extension to reply on the merits the Respondent must nevertheless, as a condition to the granting of the extension, make his views known on the number of arbitrators, and when the number has been agreed by the parties, its nomination or agreement to an arbitrator. This is so that an extension of time to answer on the merits will not lead to delay in the constitution of the Tribunal.

OTHER REFERENCES:

C.P.&P., Section 10.05, "Answer and Counterclaim".

5(3) The Answer shall be supplied to the Secretariat in the number of copies specified by article 3(1).

PRIOR TEXT: NEW

MODIFICATION: N.A.

COMMENT: This clause makes it clear that the Answer is to be officially served on the Secretariat, not the Claimant, and in the requisite number of copies.

OTHER REFERENCES:

5(4) A copy of the Answer and the documents annexed thereto shall be communicated by the Secretariat to the Claimant.

PRIOR TEXT: Article 4(2), 1975 Rules

Article 4(2)

A copy of the Answer and of the documents annexed thereto, if any, shall be communicated to the Claimant for his information.

MODIFICATION: *Communication of the Answer to the Claimant is to be made "by the Secretariat".*

COMMENT: The revised subsection, consistent with Article 5(3), makes clear that the official communication of the Answer to the Claimant, and the date thereof, is based on delivery by the Secretariat. In addition, the clause informs the Respondent that it is not required to send or serve a copy of the Answer on the Claimant and that this function is to be carried out by the Secretariat.

OTHER REFERENCES:

5(5) Any counterclaim(s) made by the Respondent shall be filed with its Answer and shall provide:

    a) a description of the nature and circumstances of the dispute giving rise to the counterclaim(s); and

    b) a statement of the relief sought, including, to the extent possible, an indication of any amount(s) counterclaimed.

PRIOR TEXT: Article 5(1), 1975 Rules

Article 5(1)

If the Defendant wishes to make a counter-claim, he shall file the same with the Secretariat, at the same time as his Answer as provided for in Article 4.

    a) NEW

    b) NEW

MODIFICATION: The revised article provides that Respondent's counterclaim shall include: "a) a description of the nature and circumstances of the dispute giving rise to its counterclaim(s); and b) a statement of the relief sought, including, to the extent possible, an indication of any amount(s) counterclaimed."

COMMENT: Information required to be submitted with a counterclaim is consistent with that required to be filed with a claim as set out in Article 4(3).

The requirement to state the relief sought and, to the extent possible, "an indication of any amount(s) counterclaimed" is useful to the Court in determining (when it must make this choice) whether a sole arbitrator or a three man tribunal should be constituted, and the amount of the advance on costs (*see* Article 30).

Article 30(5) of the new Rules provides that when a party claims a right of set-off against any claim or counterclaim asserted against, the Court will take this set-off claim into account when setting the advance on costs "in the same way as a separate claim insofar as it may require the Arbitral Tribunal to consider additional matters". Accordingly, the Working Party considered whether a Respondent should be required to specify and quantify any claim of set-off with its Answer and Counterclaim (with the possible consequences of losing a right of set-off if such was not made prior to and included in the Terms of Reference (*see* Article 18). Because of the differing treatment of set-off under national laws, and the possible interference of a right to assert a defense of a right of set-off not asserted as a counterclaim, which, under some laws may be made at any time, the Rules were not revised to require the specific pleading at the time of filing the Answer.

OTHER REFERENCES:

C.P.&P., Section 10.05, "Answer and Counterclaim".

See ICC Arbitration No. 5713 of 1989, 15 *Yearbook* 70 (1990) (discussing differences between set-off and counterclaim).

5(6) The Claimant shall file a Reply to any counterclaim within 30 days from the date of receipt of the counterclaim(s) communicated by the Secretariat. The Secretariat may grant the Claimant an extension of time for filing the Reply.

PRIOR TEXT: Article 5(2), 1975 Rules

Article 5(2)

It shall be open to the Claimant to file a Reply with the Secretariat within 30 days from the date when the counterclaim was communicated to him.

MODIFICATION: The revised Rule provides that "The Secretariat may grant the Claimant an extension of time for filing the Reply". In addition, the method for the communication of the claims to the Claimant is incorporated, consistent with Article 5(4).

COMMENT: It was deemed advisable to spell out the Secretariat's power to grant the Claimant an extension of time to reply to a counterclaim, in conjunction with its power to grant an extension to the Respondent to file an Answer. Consistent with Article 5(2) of the 1998 Rules, no limitation of this power to "exceptional circumstances" was included. *See* Article 5(2), 1988 Rules.

There is no requirement for a Reply to be filed to any counterclaim and the Respondent's defense can be spelled out later in the proceedings. A party wishing to have its opposition to any counterclaim recorded in the Terms of Reference can make its position known even subsequent to the time for Reply, or any extension thereof. Pursuant to Article 18, the Terms of Reference are drawn up in "light of [the] most recent submissions" of the parties.

OTHER REFERENCES:

The Court proposed that "In exceptional circumstances, the Claimant may apply to the Secretariat for an extension of time" be added for consistency with Article 4 and the Secretariat's practice.

Article 6
Effect of the Arbitration Agreement

6(1) Where the parties have agreed to submit to arbitration under the Rules, they shall be deemed to have submitted *ipso facto* to the Rules in effect on the date of commencement of the arbitration proceedings unless they have agreed to submit to the Rules in effect on the date of their arbitration agreement.

PRIOR TEXT: Article 8(1), 1975 Rules

Article 8(1)

Where the parties have agreed to submit to arbitration by the International Chamber of Commerce, they shall be deemed thereby to have submitted ipso facto to the present Rules.

MODIFICATION: The phrase "under the Rules" replaces "by the International Chamber of Commerce". "Present rules" is amended to read "the Rules in effect" thereafter followed by "on the date of the commencement of the arbitration proceedings unless they have agreed to submit to the Rules in effect on the date of their arbitration agreement".

COMMENT: The provision in the prior Rules that the parties shall be deemed to "have submitted *ipso facto* to the present Rules" is ambiguous since it is unclear whether the "present Rules" include modifications to those Rules which have occurred after the agreement to arbitrate or even after arbitral proceedings have commenced. The provision in the new Rules confirms the Court's prior practice: unless the parties have agreed otherwise, the Rules to be applied are those in effect on the date of commencement of the arbitration. Article 6(1), on its face, only provides one other possibility: where the parties have agreed that the Rules to be applied are those in effect on the date of the agreement to arbitrate, that agreement will be applied. In the unlikely event that the parties agree to apply the Rules in effect on some other date, for instance on the date of signature of the Terms of Reference, or as modified during the course of the proceedings, the parties' agreement should be complied with. This is consistent with the spirit of the new Rules which encourages agreements of the parties on procedural matters.

In order to promote uniformity in current ICC arbitral practice, the court has instructed the Secretariat, where the arbitration agreement calls for the application of a prior version of the Rules, to invite the parties to consider the possibility of coming to an agreement on the application of the new Rules.

The 1998 Rules entered into effect on January 1, 1998 pursuant to the decision of the Council of the International Chamber of Commerce. Accordingly, in the absence of specific agreement to the contrary, all arbitrations commenced from January 1, 1998 onwards are subject to the 1998 Rules.

OTHER REFERENCES:

C.P.&P., Section 10.03, "Which edition of the ICC Rules applies?" describes the prior practice of the Court and national court decisions dealing with the issue.

The Court recommended that the following proviso be inserted after the first sentence of subsection 1, in order to eliminate uncertainties that may arise when the Rules are revised: "Unless the parties otherwise agree, the applicable Rules shall be those in force on the date of receipt of the Request for Arbitration by the Secretariat of the Court". This addition is in accordance with practice as from 1975.

The practice of the Court following modification to the 1975 Rules entering into force on January 1, 1988 is described in a letter of November 20, 1987 from the Secretary General of the Court to all parties, counsel and arbitrators involved in ICC Arbitration proceedings. The letter is reprinted in Appendix II of C.P. & P.

In ICC Arbitration N° 5621 of 1992, 8 *ICC Bull.* N° 1, 52 (1997) the Arbitral Tribunal applied the 1988 modifications to the 1975 Rules to an arbitration where the agreement was concluded in 1980 but the arbitration commenced in 1988 (the relevant modification was the new Article 2 (12) which provided that in case of replacement of an arbitrator the new arbitrator would determine to what extent prior proceedings had to be repeated).

For an earlier court case on the issue, *see* Mobil Oil Indonesia, Inc. v. Asenora Oil (Indonesia) 392 NYS 2d 614 (1977) when the arbitral tribunal decided, and was sustained by the court, that the 1975 version of the ICC Rules would apply even though the 1955 Rules were in effect at the date of the arbitration agreement.

6(2) If the Respondent does not file an Answer, as provided by Article 5, or if any party raises one or more pleas concerning the existence, validity or scope of the arbitration agreement, the Court may decide, without prejudice to the admissibility or merits of the plea or pleas, that the arbitration shall proceed if it is *prima facie* satisfied that an arbitration agreement under the Rules may exist. In such a case, any decision as to the jurisdiction of the Arbitral Tribunal shall be taken by the Arbitral Tribunal itself. If the Court is not so satisfied, the parties shall be notified that the arbitration cannot proceed. In such a case, any party retains the right to ask any court having jurisdiction whether or not there is a binding arbitration agreement.

PRIOR TEXT: Article 8(3), 1975 Rules; Article 7, 1975 Rules, Article 12, 1980 Internal Rules

Article 8(3)

Should one of the parties raise one or more pleas concerning the existence or validity of the agreement to arbitrate, and should the International Court of Arbitration be satisfied of the prima facie existence of such an agreement, the

Court may, without prejudice to the admissibility or merits of the plea or pleas, decide that the arbitration shall proceed. In such a case any decision as to the arbitrator's jurisdiction shall be taken by the arbitrator himself.

Article 7
Absence of the agreement to arbitrate

Where there is no prima facie agreement between the parties to arbitrate or where there is an agreement but it does not specify the International Chamber of Commerce, and if the Defendant doe not file an Answer within the period of 30 days provided by paragraph 1 of Article 4 or refuses arbitration by the International Chamber of Commerce, the Claimant shall be informed that the arbitration cannot proceed.

Article 12, Internal Rules
Absence of an arbitration agreement

Where there is no prima facie arbitration agreement between the parties or where there is an agreement but it does not specify the ICC, the Secretariat draws the attention of the Claimant to the provisions laid down in Article 7 of the Rules of Arbitration. The Claimant is entitled to require the decision to be taken by the International Court of Arbitration.

This decision is of an administrative nature. If the Court decides that the arbitration solicited by the Claimant cannot proceed, the parties retain the right to ask the competent jurisdiction whether or not they are bound by an arbitration agreement in the light of the law applicable.

If the Court considered prima facie that the proceedings may take place, the arbitrator appointed has the duty to decide as to his own jurisdiction and, where such jurisdiction exists, as to the merits of the dispute.

MODIFICATION: Article 6(2) modifies and consolidates the provisions of prior Articles 7 and 8(3) concerning the determination of the Court prima facie that there exists an agreement to arbitrate and that the arbitrators should proceed without prejudice to the Arbitral Tribunal's power, if constituted, to make a final decision as to any issues of jurisdiction. The Article also incorporates the provision of Article 12 of the 1980 Internal Rules that where the Court has not prima facie been satisfied that an arbitration agreement exists, it will decide that the arbitration shall not proceed, such a decision being administrative in nature. The issue of the existence of an agreement to arbitrate may then be brought by the disappointed party to any court having jurisdiction.

COMMENT: The provision that, where the Court has ordered an arbitration to proceed, "any decision as to the jurisdiction of the Arbitral Tribunal shall be taken by the Arbitral Tribunal itself" reflects the incorporation into the Rules of the principle of *compétence-compétence*, according to which the arbitrator has power to determine his own jurisdiction.

The companion notion of the autonomy of the arbitration clause, - which implies that the arbitrator retains jurisdiction to determine the merits of a dispute under the agreement despite the agreement's alleged invalidity or termination - is provided for in the new Article 6(4). The Court's power to make this preliminary decision, of an administrative nature, of whether to forward the matter to an Arbitral Tribunal, now arises either where the Respondent does not file an Answer or where one of the parties raises a plea concerning the existence, validity or scope of the arbitration agreement. Article 12 of the 1980 Internal Rules calling for the Secretariat, *sua sponte*, to advise the Claimant that, *prima facie*, no arbitration agreement exists, has been eliminated from the 1998 International Rules. Such preliminary determination very frequently involved a request for the Court to redetermine the issue with significant waste of time. Under the revised Rules, the Court will take steps to constitute a tribunal and to send the file to the Arbitral Tribunal once the Claimant has fulfilled all the requirements of the Request and the requisite advance on costs. It will make a *prima facie* determination only if the Respondent fails to file an Answer, or raises in its Answer or otherwise, jurisdictional issues concerning the arbitration agreement.

Article 7 of the 1975 Rules and Article 12 of the 1980 Internal Rules both provided for the case "[w]here there is no *prima facie* agreement between the parties to arbitrate". The revision provides that the arbitration shall proceed if the Court "is *prima facie* satisfied that an arbitration agreement . . . may exist". The editorial change is purposeful. The term "*prima facie* agreement" was a misnomer since most issues of jurisdiction will arise precisely when the formal or "*prima facie*" existence of the arbitration agreement is put in doubt. The kinds of issues which arise are whether an existing agreement may be extended to non-signatories, or to a dispute between the parties not specifically provided for in their agreement. What is really intended is that the arbitration shall proceed if there is *prima facie* evidence of an agreement to arbitrate, which could reasonably be made out before the Arbitral Tribunal. Another way to put it is that the Court should be convinced that an arbitration agreement "may arguably exist". This concept is included in the requirement that the Court shall be "*prima facie* satisfied that an arbitration agreement . . . may exist".

The ICC Rules do not contain any express provision concerning the "arbitrability" of disputes. This determination is to be made by the Arbitral Tribunal as part of its mission to take a decision as to its jurisdiction, in the face of any plea concerning the "existence, validity or scope of the arbitration agreement". The Court, in pursuit of its *prima facie* determination mission, will only look for the existence of an arbitration agreement and not investigate the arbitrability of the dispute.

The 1998 Rules, like the 1975 Rules, do not contain any requirement that objections to the jurisdiction of the Arbitral Tribunal or the arbitrability of any claim be made at any particular time (compare *e.g.* UNCITRAL Rules, of which Article 21.3 requires that a plea that the Arbitral Tribunal does not have any jurisdiction be made not later than the statement of defense). Accordingly, under the Rules, such defenses may be raised throughout the proceedings. This might conflict, however, with applicable national procedural law (requiring that jurisdictional defenses be raised at the outset of the proceeding *e.g.* Article 186.2

of the Swiss Private International Law Act, 1987) which should be consulted. Compare also the provisions of Article 33, "Waiver", of the 1998 Rules.

OTHER REFERENCES:

C.P. & P. Section 11.01, "The Court of Arbitration's preliminary determination of "prima facie" agreement to arbitrate" and Section 11.02, "Procedure for raising jurisdictional issues before the Court of Arbitration" describe the Court's practice on *"prima facie"* determinations, and the testing of the Court's power in national courts. Section 11.03, "Arbitrator's authority to determine his own jurisdiction" describes the ICC arbitration precedents. *See also* Section 5.07, "Arbitrability".

For a much-cited arbitral award describing the power of an arbitrator to determine his own jurisdiction, *see* ICC Award N° 1526, 1974 *JDI* 915 (Commentary by Derains, regretting that the arbitrator felt compelled to refer to numerous national procedural laws as precedent, and did not rely more on the express provisions of the ICC Rules).

See ICC Arbitration N° 6437 of 1990, 8 *ICC Bull.* N° 1, 63 (determination of issue of jurisdiction by sole arbitrator. Non-application of any rule of national procedural law. Reliance on terms of New York Convention which had been ratified by all countries having ties to the parties and the dispute).

On the impact under national law of a provision that jurisdictional questions are for the arbitral tribunal, *see dictum* First Options of Chicago v. Kaplan, 115 S. Ct. 1920 (1995) (if the parties agreed to submit arbitrability to the arbitrator, " the court should give considerable leeway to the arbitrator"). *See also* Paine Webber v. Elahi, 87 F.3d 589 (1st Cir. 1996) (applies above-cited First Options *dictum* to language in the NASD Code of Arbitration Procedure providing for arbitrators to "interpret and determine the applicability of all provisions under this Code"; arbitrators not courts should determine preconditions to arbitration). *Contrast* Merrill Lynch v. Cohen, 62 F.2d 381 (11th Cir. 1995) (preconditions for courts not arbitrators).

In Apollo v. Berg, 886 F. 2d 469 (1st Cir. 1989), the Court of Appeals relied in part on Article 8 of the 1975 Rules to limit its own power to review the validity of an arbitration agreement. *See also* Daiei Inc. V. United States Shoe Corporation, 755 F. Supp. 229 (D. Hawaii 1991) (agreement to ICC Rules constitutes an agreement that issues of arbitrability are for the arbitrator).

Article 21(1) UNCITRAL Rules, provides for *compétence -compétence* in the following terms:

> The arbitral tribunal shall have the power to rule on objections that it has no jurisdiction, including any objection with respect to the existence or validity of the arbitration clause or of the separate arbitration agreement.

Article 15 (1) of the American Arbitration Association International Rules provides: "The tribunal shall have the power to rule on its own jurisdiction, including any objections with respect to the existence, scope or validity of the arbitration agreement".

Article 14.1 of the LCIA Rules provides: "The Tribunal shall have the power to rule on its own jurisdiction, including any objections with respect to the existence or validity of the arbitration agreement".

See E. Schwartz, "The Domain of Arbitration and Issues of Arbitrability: The View from the ICC", 9 *ICSID Rev. (For. Inv. L.J.)* 17 (1994).

See Y. Takla, "Non-ICC arbitration clauses and clauses derogating from the ICC Rules", 7 *ICC Bull.* No. 2, 7 (1996).

See A. Dimolitsa, "Issues concerning the existence, validity and effectiveness of the arbitration agreement", 7 *ICC Bull.* No. 2, 14 (1996).

See T. Klein, "Disagreement on the scope of the arbitration clause", 7 *ICC Bull.* No. 2, 24 (1996).

See J. Benglia, "Inaccurate References to the ICC", 7 *ICC Bull.* No. 2, 11 (1996).

See J.E. Cremades, "Problems that Arise from changes Affecting One of the Signatories to the Arbitration Clause", 7 *ICC Bull.* No. 332 (1996).

6(3) If any of the parties refuses or fails to take part in the arbitration or any stage thereof, the arbitration shall proceed notwithstanding such refusal or failure.

PRIOR TEXT: Article 8(2), 1975 Rules

Article 8(2)

If one of the parties refuses or fails to take part in the arbitration, the arbitration shall proceed notwithstanding such refusal or failure.

MODIFICATION: "If one of the parties" is replaced by "If any of the parties" in the new article. The words "or any stage thereof" are inserted following the reference to failing to take part in the arbitration.

COMMENT: The change is consistent with the language used throughout the new text of the Rules.

OTHER REFERENCES:

C. P.& P. Section 10.06, "Failure or refusal to answer: ex parte proceedings".

See also Articles 8(3), 8(4), 1998 Rules concerning the appointment by the Court of an arbitrator in the case of failure by a party to nominate an arbitrator.

When a party fails to participate in the proceedings or fails to file defensive pleadings within permitted time periods, the Tribunal will proceed to adjudicate the merits of the case without taking this failure as acquiescence in the other party's claims or allegations. *See* ICC Arbitration N° 6670 of 1992 *JDI* 1010, obs.

J-J Arnaldez; ICC Arbitration N° 7153, 1992 *JDI* 1005, obs. D. Hascher; ICC Arbitration N°6149, 1990 3 ICC Collection 315.

6(4) Unless otherwise agreed, the Arbitral Tribunal shall not cease to have jurisdiction by reason of any claim that the contract is null and void or allegation that it is non-existent provided that the Arbitral Tribunal upholds the validity of the arbitration agreement. The Arbitral Tribunal shall continue to have jurisdiction to determine the respective rights of the parties and to adjudicate their claims and pleas even though the contract itself may be non-existent or null and void.

PRIOR TEXT: Article 8(4), 1975 Rules

Article 8(4)

Unless otherwise provided, the arbitrator shall not cease to have jurisdiction by reason of any claim that the contract is null and void or allegation that it is inexistent provided that he upholds the validity of the agreement to arbitrate. He shall continue to have jurisdiction, even though the contract itself may be inexistent or null and void, to determine the respective rights of the parties and to abjudicate upon their claims and pleas.

MODIFICATION: The first sentence now begins "Unless otherwise agreed" in lieu of "Unless otherwise provided". The order of some sentences has been reversed, and "Arbitral Tribunal" replaces "it".

COMMENT: Article 6(4) of the Rules, like its predecessor Article 8(4), provides for the autonomy or severability of the arbitration clause. ICC arbitrators are thus specifically empowered, in accordance with the established principles of international arbitration, to exercise jurisdiction to determine the respective obligations of parties pursuant to an agreement containing an ICC arbitration clause, despite arguments concerning the invalidity or termination of the principal agreement. *See* commentary under Article 6(2), *supra.*

OTHER REFERENCES:

C.P. & P., Section 5.04, "Autonomy of the arbitration clause" states that "[a]cceptance of this autonomy of the arbitration clause is a conceptual cornerstone of international arbitration" and sets out a number of the arbitral and national court decisions dealing with the issue.

See also Reisman, Craig, Park and Paulsson, *International Commercial Arbitration: Cases, Materials and Notes on the Resolution of International Business Disputes* (Foundation Press: 1997), Chapter 3, "Arbitrability", Chapter 6, "Preliminary Decisions".

See S. Schwebel, "The Severability of the Arbitration Agreement" in *International Arbitration: Three Salient Problems* 1, at 60 (1987) (Grotius Publications, Cambridge).

THE ARBITRAL TRIBUNAL

Article 7
General Provisions

7(1) Every arbitrator must be and remain independent of the parties involved in the arbitration.

PRIOR TEXT: First paragraph of Article 2(7), 1975 Rules

2(7) Every arbitrator appointed or confirmed by the Court must be and remain independent of the parties involved in the arbitration

MODIFICATION: The defining term "appointed or confirmed by the Court" is omitted.

COMMENT: The independence required of the arbitrators, whether sole arbitrators, presiding arbitrators, or party-nominated arbitrators is a key characteristic of ICC arbitration. The issue of independence, or lack thereof, has been raised most frequently in the case of party-nominated arbitrators, alleged to have a financial or similar relationship with the party nominating them. Lack of independence is a ground, but not the only ground, for challenge or disqualification of an arbitrator, *see* Rule 11(1), *infra.*

Most modern institutional arbitration rules for international arbitration provide that arbitrators should be independent and impartial.

Indeed, Article 15(2) of the Rules, added by the 1998 revision, provides that the Arbitral Tribunal "shall act fairly and impartially". One of the reasons given for not modifying the Rules to provide, at the outset, that an arbitrator must be independent and impartial was the argument that lack of independence was an objective status, subject to factual determination, whereas partiality was most frequently revealed by conduct.   Under the Rules, the Court has, in its confirmation process, the unique role of making an early judgment about the arbitrator's aptitude to serve. To confirm arbitrators, the Court, based on the arbitrators' statement required under Article 7(2), will have on hand sufficient material to make a reasoned judgment about an arbitrator's independence.   The requirement of impartiality requires more subjective judgments and frequently is only revealed by an arbitrator's conduct which can be brought to the attention of the Court in challenge proceedings.

The concepts of independence and impartiality are closely linked and the importance of the fact that the Rules emphasize the independence rather than the impartiality of arbitrators should not be over-estimated. In fact, the reason for requiring the independence of an arbitrator is to assure that the arbitrator can act fairly and impartially as is required by his function.

OTHER REFERENCES:

C.P. & P., Section 13.03, "Independence required of arbitrator" describes the Court's practice regarding the independence of arbitrators. *See also* Section 13.04 "Arbitrator's duty of disclosure" and Section 13.05 "Grounds for Challenge".

The independence of arbitrators in the context of ICC arbitration has been the source of frequent and recent writings: *See* D. Hascher, "ICC Practice in relation to the Appointment, Confirmation, Challenge and Replacement of Arbitrators", 6 *ICC Bull.* no. 2, pp. 5-6, 13-16 (1995), Dossiers of the Institute; "The Arbitral Process and Independence of Arbitrators", ICC Pub. No. 472 (1993).

See AAA International Rules, Article 7: "Arbitrators acting under these rules shall be impartial and independent".

See LCIA Rules, Article 3: "All arbitrators (whether or not nominated by the parties) conducting an arbitration under the Rules shall be and remain at all times wholly independent and impartial, and shall not act as advocates for any party. . . ".

See WIPO Rules, Article 22 (a): "Each arbitrator shall be impartial and independent".

See S. Bond: "The Selection of ICC Arbitrators and the Requirement of Independence", *4 Arb. Int'l.* 300 (1988).

See IDI v. Fertilizer Corp. of India. 530 F. Supp. 542 (S.D.Ohio 1982), where an arbitrator had represented the party that nominated him but had failed to disclose the link. Enforcement of the award was resisted on the basis of "public policy." Because the court gave public policy a narrow reading, it refused to deny recognition to the award. Under the relevant ICC rules (the 1955 version), arbitrator's independence was arguably implicit in the spirit of the rules, but not contained in any concrete provision. In connection with the possibility of a challenge to an award where the arbitrator lacks independence, and where the Rules specifically require the arbitrator's independence, note that New York Convention Article V(1)(d) provides for refusal of recognition to an award if the "arbitration procedure was not in accordance with the agreement of the parties".

7(2) Before appointment or confirmation, a prospective arbitrator shall sign a statement of independence and disclose in writing to the Secretariat any facts or circumstances which might be of such a nature as to call into question the arbitrator's independence in the eyes of the parties. The Secretariat shall provide such information to the parties in writing and fix a time limit for any comments from them.

PRIOR TEXT: Second paragraph of Article 2(7), 1975 Rules

Before appointment or confirmation by the Court, a prospective arbitrator shall disclose in writing to the Secretary General of the Court any facts or circumstances which might be of such a nature as to call into question the arbitrator's independence in the eyes of the parties. Upon receipt of such information, the Secretary General of the Court shall provide it to the parties in writing and fix a time-limit for any comments from them.

MODIFICATION: The revised rule requires the prospective arbitrator to sign a statement of independence and to fill out a written disclosure form. The "Secretariat" and not the "Secretary General" "shall provide such information to the parties" at the appropriate times, not necessarily "on receipt of the information" which has been eliminated. The substitution of the "Secretariat" for the "Secretary General" reflects the fact that each arbitration is assigned a member of the Secretariat (a "counsel") who follows the file and handles such administrative issues.

COMMENT: The requirement of signature of a statement of independence accords with current practice. The form of the disclosure in writing brings to the attention of the arbitrator possible conflicts with his independence and requires him to take a position thereon prior to signing the statement of independence. The form permits the prospective arbitrator to make a statement of independence without reservation or with reservation in which latter case the circumstances of the reservation are brought to the attention of the parties.

The various correspondence regarding the issue of independence is an administrative duty of the Secretariat. Reference to the Secretary General has therefore been eliminated to reflect practice since the Secretariat functions under the supervision and control of the Secretary General (*see* Article 1(5), *supra*). The modified text reflects no real change.

The obligation to disclose any facts or circumstances which might call into question the arbitrator's independence "in the eyes of the parties" calls for the application of a very broad notion of independence, thus including also, it would seem, notions of impartiality, *See* Comment at Article 7(1).

OTHER REFERENCES:

C.P. & P. Section 13.04, "Arbitrator's duty of disclosure".

See Secretariat of the ICC Court, "Arbitrator's Declaration of Acceptance and Statement of Independence", 6 *ICC Bull*. No. 2, 77 (1995).

UNCITRAL Rules, Article 9 provides that an arbitrator shall disclose "any circumstances likely to give rise to justifiable doubts as to his impartiality or independence". Article 10 provides that "Any arbitrator may be challenged if circumstances exist that give rise to justifiable doubts as to the arbitrator's impartiality or independence".

See AAA International Rules, Article 7: ". . . Prior to accepting appointment, a prospective arbitrator shall disclose to the administrator any circumstance likely to give rise to justifiable doubts as to the arbitrator's impartiality or independence."

See LCIA Rules, Articles 3.1: ". . . In any event every arbitrator shall sign a declaration to the effect that there are no circumstances likely to give rise to any justified doubts as to his impartiality or independence, and that he will forthwith disclose any . . .".

See WIPO Rules, Article 22 (b): "Each prospective arbitrator shall, before accepting appointment, disclose to the parties, the Center and any other arbitrator who has already been appointed any circumstances that might give rise to justifiable doubt as to the arbitrator's impartiality or independence, or confirm in writing that no such circumstances exist".

See IBA Ethics, Article 5.1: "When approached with a view to appointment, a prospective arbitrator should make sufficient enquiries in order to inform himself whether there may be any justifiable doubts regarding his impartiality or independence; whether he is competent to determine the issues in dispute; and whether he is able to give the arbitration the time and attention required"

7(3) An arbitrator shall immediately disclose in writing to the Secretariat and to the parties any facts or circumstances of a similar nature which may arise during the arbitration.

PRIOR TEXT: Third paragraph of Article 2(7), 1975 Rules

An arbitrator shall immediately disclose in writing to the Secretary General of the Court and the parties any facts or circumstances of a similar nature which may arise between the arbitrator's appointment or confirmation by the Court and the notification of the final award.

MODIFICATIONS: The new Article 7(3) refers to the Secretariat in place of the Secretary General. The other modification is the simplification of the phrase "between the arbitrator's appointment or confirmation by the Court and the notification of the final award".

COMMENT: *See* 2nd paragraph of Comment at Article 7(2).

OTHER REFERENCES:

7(4) The decisions of the Court as to the appointment, confirmation, challenge or replacement of an arbitrator shall be final and the reasons for such decisions shall not be communicated.

PRIOR TEXT: Article 2(13), 1975 Rules

Decisions of the Court as to the appointment, confirmation, challenge or replacement of an arbitrator shall be final.

The reasons for decisions by the Court as to the appointment, confirmation, challenge or replacement of an arbitrator on the grounds that he is not fulfilling his functions in accordance with the Rules or within the prescribed time-limits, shall not be communicated.

MODIFICATION: The new article has been simplified.

COMMENT: The role of the Court concerning appointment, confirmation, challenge or replacement is administrative in nature and is intended to be summary and expeditious. It is part of the supervisory function which the parties accept by agreeing to the Rules.

OTHER REFERENCES:

C.P. & P., Section 13.01, "Rejection of nomination, challenge, and disqualification", Section 13.02, "The Court's standards and their sources".

The Court's decisions are of an administrative nature; *see* ICC Arbitration N° 6519 of 1991, 1991 *JDI* 1065, obs. Derains.

7(5) By accepting to serve, every arbitrator undertakes to carry out his responsibilities in accordance with these Rules.

PRIOR TEXT: NEW

MODIFICATION: N.A.

COMMENT: This important change, added at the Commission's meeting of 27 February 1997 (ICC Doc. No. 420/360, p. 2), is intended to make clear that an arbitrator's responsibility to serve extends throughout the arbitration. The arbitrator's duties include an obligation of availability and to proceed with diligence so that an award may be rendered in a timely fashion. As is now expressly provided by Article 12(1) of the Rules, the arbitrator remains under these obligations unless and until he has been discharged of them by a decision of the Court. An arbitrator may not be relieved of these responsibilities simply by tendering his resignation. The resignation must be accepted by the Court. The modification should be helpful in dealing with a case where (usually towards the end of an arbitration) an arbitrator either ceases attending arbitral deliberations or proffers his resignation. The arbitrator may be reminded of his obligation to continue to serve. *See also* Article 12(5) concerning the power of the Court to order that the arbitration shall continue with the remaining two arbitrators (a "truncated tribunal") where, after the closing of the proceedings, an arbitrator has died or been removed by the Court.

OTHER REFERENCES:

Rules, Article 12(1): "An arbitrator shall be replaced upon his death, upon the acceptance by the Court of the arbitrator's resignation, upon acceptance by the Court of a challenge or upon the request of all the parties".

See WIPO Rules Article 23, Availability, Acceptance and Notification

> a) each arbitrator shall, by accepting appointment, be deemed to have undertaken to make available sufficient time to enable the arbitration to be conducted and completed expeditiously.

See S. Schwebel, "The Validity of an Arbitral Award Rendered by a Truncated Tribunal", 6 *ICC Bull.* No. 2, 19 (1995).

See E. Schwartz, "The Rights and Duties of ICC Arbitrators", in The Status of the Arbitrator, *ICC Bull.* (Special Supplement, 1995) 67.

7(6) Insofar as the parties have not provided otherwise, the Arbitral Tribunal shall be constituted in accordance with the provisions of Articles 8, 9 and 10.

PRIOR TEXT: Second sentence of Article 2(1), 1975 Rules

Insofar as the parties shall not have provided otherwise, it [the Court] *appoints, or confirms the appointments of, arbitrators in accordance with the provisions of this Article*

MODIFICATION.   Article 7(6) provides that the Court will constitute the Tribunal in accordance with "the provisions of Articles 8, 9 and 10" which contain the same subject matter as Article 2 of the 1975 Rules.

COMMENT: The addition of the new reference to Articles 8, 9 and 10 conforms to the change in organization of these Articles dedicated to the Arbitral Tribunal. The article confirms the power of the parties to make special agreements for the appointment of the Arbitral Tribunal in which case the requirements of Article 8 ("Number of Arbitrators"), Article 9 ("Appointment and Confirmation of the Arbitrators") and Article 10 ("Multiple Parties") do not apply. In appropriate cases this would permit the parties to agree to a number of arbitrators other than one or three. It would also permit them to agree to the appointment of arbitrators by a third party other than the Court.

The Article reflects the general intent of the revision of the Rules: to respect the parties' special agreements on procedural matters.

Despite this confirmation of parties' power to make special arrangements for the appointment of the Arbitral Tribunal the Court retains a general supervisory power even over such special arrangements, as well as over other procedural agreements by the parties, pursuant to Article 35 ("General Rule"). Under prior practice the Court reserved the right to and would formally take action concerning arbitrators who were named by a special agreement between the parties. Presumably it will continue to do so under the 1998 Rules. Under the formula used under the 1975 Rules the Court "confirms" arbitrators nominated by the parties, "appoints" arbitrators of its own choice and "takes note" of appointments made by special agreement of the parties (*see* Articles 8(3) and 8(4), *infra*). *See* ICC Arbitration No. 2321 of 1974, 1 ICC Collection 8 (where the parties to an ICC arbitration had agreed that the sole arbitrator should be appointed by another appointing authority (FIDIC) but had that authority refused to appoint, the ICC Court would make the appointment, and the arbitrator confirmed his jurisdiction).

The clause in Article 7(6) "Insofar as the parties shall not have provided otherwise . . . " represents the only affirmation in the Rules that the parties maintain absolute liberty in their choice of how the Tribunal will be constituted. It is important to note, however, that their choice must conform to the national laws under which the arbitration is being governed. The choice must also respect the conditions of Articles 7(1)-(5), which constitute non-waivable fundamental public policy of the ICC Rules.

OTHER REFERENCES:

See Article 10, 1998 Rules, "Multiple Parties".

See S. Bond, "The Constitution of the Arbitral Tribunal", *ICC Bull.* Supp. 22 (1997).

Article 8
Number of Arbitrators

8(1) The disputes shall be decided by a sole arbitrator or by three arbitrators.

PRIOR TEXT: First sentence of Article 2(2), 1975 Rules

Article 2(2)

The disputes may be settled by a sole arbitrator or by three arbitrators.

MODIFICATION: "[M]ay be" is replaced by "shall be". "[S]ettled" is replaced by "decided".

COMMENT: No substantive change is made in the provision of the 1975 Rules which, by indicating that arbitration is to take place either before a sole arbitrator or a tribunal of three arbitrators, appears to rule out arbitration before a greater number of arbitrators where there is no agreement as to the number of arbitrators and the Court must make this choice. Where, however, the parties have specifically agreed to another number of arbitrators the Court has discretion to approve such an arrangement (*see* Article 7(6), *supra*). Several ICC arbitrations before tribunals composed of more than three arbitrators, as specifically agreed by the parties, have taken place in the past. Since the new Rules tend to favor approving procedures specifically agreed to by the parties, the possibility for parties to make special arrangements for the number of arbitrators is enhanced. The Court retains discretion not to approve the constitution of tribunals which would be unworkable or which would violate mandatory laws in effect at the place of arbitration.

OTHER REFERENCES:

C.P.&P., Section 12.02, "Number of Arbitrators".

8(2) Where the parties have not agreed upon the number of arbitrators, the Court shall appoint a sole arbitrator, save where it appears to the Court that the dispute is such as to warrant the appointment of three arbitrators. In such case, the Claimant shall nominate an arbitrator within a period of 15 days from the receipt of the notification of the decision of the Court, and the Respondent shall nominate an arbitrator within a period of 15 days from the receipt of the notification of the nomination made by the Claimant.

PRIOR TEXT: Article 2(5), 1975 Rules.

Article 2(5)

Where the parties have not agreed upon the number of arbitrators, the Court shall appoint a sole arbitrator, save where it appears to the Court that the dispute is such as to warrant the appointment of three arbitrators. In such a case, the parties shall each have a period of 30 days in which to nominate an arbitrator.

MODIFICATION: The second sentence is modified so that where the Court, ruling in the absence of party agreement on the issue, has determined that a three person tribunal is appropriate, "the Claimant shall nominate an arbitrator within a period of 15 days from the receipt of the notification of the decision of the Court and the Respondent shall nominate an arbitrator within a period of 15 days from the receipt of the notification of the nomination made by the Claimant".

COMMENT: Where the parties have agreed to a three person tribunal, the Rules provide that the Claimant shall name its arbitrator in the Request for Arbitration and the Respondent shall name its arbitrator thirty days thereafter, thus having the opportunity to make its decision with knowledge of the arbitrator named by its adversary. This defensive advantage was considered to be a normal attribute of the arbitral process and it has been extended to the case where the constitution of a three man tribunal is based on the decision of the Court. The time for each party to appoint its arbitrator has been reduced to 15 days, thus maintaining a 30 day period for the two choices.

OTHER REFERENCES:

C.P.&P. Section 12.02, "Number of Arbitrators".

See C. Imhoos, "The ICC Arbitral Process, Part I: Constitution of the Arbitral Tribunal", 2 *ICC Bull.* No. 2, 3 (1991).

8(3) Where the parties have agreed that the dispute shall be settled by a sole arbitrator, they may, by agreement, nominate the sole arbitrator for confirmation. If the parties fail to nominate a sole arbitrator within 30 days from the date when the Claimant's Request for Arbitration has been received by the other party, or within such additional time as may be allowed by the Secretariat, the sole arbitrator shall be appointed by the Court.

PRIOR TEXT: Article 2(3), 1975 Rules

Article 2(3)

Where the parties have agreed that the disputes shall be settled by a sole arbitrator, they may, by agreement, nominate him for confirmation by the Court. If the parties fail so to nominate a sole arbitrator within 30 days from the date when the Claimant's Request for Arbitration has been communicated to the other party, the sole arbitrator shall be appointed by the Court.

MODIFICATION: The revised article refers to the Secretariat's power to allow additional time for the nomination of the arbitrator.

COMMENT: The reference to the Secretariat's power to allow additional time for nomination of the arbitrator is consistent with Article 5, Article 8, and the Secretariat's practice. The Secretariat has in the past very frequently extended this 30 day time limit, and an express provision for this extension is consistent with the Rules.

Note that the agreement that the dispute shall be settled by a sole arbitrator may be made in the arbitration agreement or by subsequent agreement by the parties. Frequently arbitration clauses provide for arbitration by three arbitrators but the dispute which arises under it turns out to be a small one where it would be uneconomical to have a three person tribunal. In such circumstances the parties should try to modify the agreement and provide for a sole arbitrator. The Secretariat encourages the parties to make this kind of post-dispute agreement.

OTHER REFERENCES:

C.P.&P., Section 12.03, "Appointment of Sole Arbitrator or Chairman".

8(4) Where the dispute is to be referred to three arbitrators, each party shall nominate in the Request and the Answer, respectively, one arbitrator for confirmation by the Court. If a party fails to nominate an arbitrator, the appointment shall be made by the Court. The third arbitrator, who will act as chairman of the Arbitral Tribunal, shall be appointed by the Court, unless the parties have agreed upon another procedure for such appointment, in which case the nomination will be subject to confirmation pursuant to Article 9. Should such procedure not result in a nomination within the time limit fixed by the parties or the Court, the third arbitrator shall be appointed by the Court.

PRIOR TEXT: Article 2(4), 1975 Rules

Article 2(4)

Where the dispute is to be referred to three arbitrators, each party shall nominate in the Request for Arbitration and the Answer thereto respectively one arbitrator for confirmation by the Court. Such person shall be independent of the party nominating him. If a party fails to nominate an arbitrator, the appointment shall be made by the Court.

The third arbitrator, who will act as Chairman of the arbitral tribunal, shall be appointed by the Court, unless the parties have provided that the arbitrators nominated by them shall agree on the third arbitrator within a fixed time limit. In such a case the Court shall confirm the appointment of such third arbitrator. Should the two arbitrators fail, within the time limit fixed by the parties or the Court, to reach agreement on the third arbitrator, he shall be appointed by the Court.

MODIFICATION: The revised article no longer requires that the person nominated be independent from the nominating party. This requirement is now addressed in Article 7(2). Other changes are editorial.

COMMENT:

OTHER REFERENCES:

See ICC Arbitration No. 6149 of 1990, 20 *Yearbook* 43, 48-49 (when one party fails to nominate an arbitrator it is for the Court to appoint an arbitrator by default and the other party may not seek appointment by a national court).

Article 9
Appointment and Confirmation of the Arbitrators

9(1) In confirming or appointing arbitrators, the Court shall consider the prospective arbitrator's nationality, residence and other relationships with the countries of which the parties or the other arbitrators are nationals and the prospective arbitrator's availability and ability to conduct the arbitration in accordance with these Rules. The same shall apply where the Secretary General confirms arbitrators pursuant to Article 9(2).

PRIOR TEXT: Article 2(1), 1975 Rules substantially modified.

Article 2

The Arbitral Tribunal

The International Court of Arbitration does not itself settle disputes. Insofar as the parties shall not have provided otherwise, it appoints, or confirms the appointments of, arbitrators in accordance with the provisions of this Article. In making or confirming such appointments, the Court shall have regard to the proposed arbitrator's nationality, residence and other relationships with the countries of which the parties or the other arbitrators are nationals.

MODIFICATION: The subsection is adapted from the third sentence of the 1975 Rules. The revised article adds that the Court must consider the prospective arbitrator's "availability and ability to conduct the arbitration in accordance with these Rules". The reference to the Secretary General has been added.

COMMENT: The addition of the reference to the availability and ability of the arbitrator to conduct the arbitration under these Rules was suggested by a number of practitioners for the purpose of clarifying the nature and extent of the Court's power to refuse to confirm an arbitrator for reasons other than for lack of independence. The Court now has the power to deny confirmation to an arbitrator as a result of his unavailability or his inability to conduct the arbitration under these Rules (*e.g.* language barriers).

The addition of a reference to the power of the Secretary General to confirm arbitrators pursuant to Article 9(2) complies with the decision to delegate to the Secretary General the power of confirmation in limited cases, with the objective of making possible the constitution of an arbitral tribunal within a period of 2 to 3 months. The Secretary General may confirm co-arbitrators, sole arbitrators, and chairmen of arbitral tribunals nominated by the parties or on the basis of their particular agreement, provided such nominees have filed a statement of independence without qualification. The Secretary General may also confirm the place of arbitration. This diminishes delays where no disputed decision need be taken and the issue is only the confirmation of a decision made by the agreement of the parties.

OTHER REFERENCES:

D. Hascher, "ICC Practice in relation to the appointment, confirmation, challenge and replacement of arbitrators", 6 *ICC Bull.* No. 2, 4 (1995).

R. Morera, "The appointment of arbitrators by the Court", 7 *ICC Bull.* No. 2, 32 (1996).

C. Imhoos, "Constituting the Arbitral Tribunal", 2 *ICC Bull.* No. 2 (1991).

S. Bond, "The Constitution of the Arbitral Tribunal," *ICC Bull.* Supp. 22 (1997).

9(2) The Secretary General may confirm as co-arbitrators, sole arbitrators and chairmen of Arbitral Tribunals persons nominated by the parties or pursuant to their particular agreements, provided they have filed a statement of independence without qualification or a qualified statement of independence has not given rise to objections. Such confirmation shall be reported to the Court at its next session. If the Secretary General considers that a co-arbitrator, sole arbitrator or chairman of an Arbitral Tribunal should not be confirmed, the matter shall be submitted to the Court.

PRIOR TEXT: NEW

MODIFICATION: N.A.

COMMENT: The provision that the Secretary General, rather than the Court, has the power to confirm arbitrators where, in effect, there is no dispute as to the nomination, is designed to save time and accelerate the arbitral process. Where this Article does not apply, issues as to confirmation of arbitrators will be decided by a three member Committee of the Court (*see* Article 1(4)). On its face, and probably due to a drafting error, the Article would permit the Secretary General to decide the issue of confirmation of an arbitrator where the arbitrator has filed an unqualified statement of independence but where nevertheless the other party objects to confirmation. In practice, no doubt, the Secretary General would refer such a case to a Committee of the Court.

OTHER REFERENCES:

9(3) Where the Court is to appoint a sole arbitrator or the chairman of an Arbitral Tribunal, it shall make the appointment upon a proposal of a National Committee of the ICC that it considers to be appropriate. If the Court does not accept the proposal made, or if the National Committee fails to make the proposal requested within the time-limit fixed by the Court, the Court may repeat its request or may request a proposal from another National Committee that it considers to be appropriate.

PRIOR TEXT: First paragraph of Article 2(6), 1975 Rules

Where the Court is to appoint a sole arbitrator or the chairman of an arbitral tribunal, it shall make the appointment after having requested a proposal from a National Committee of the ICC that it considers to be appropriate. If the Court does not accept the proposal made, or if said National Committee fails to make the proposal requested within the time-limit fixed by the Court, the Court may repeat its request or may request a proposal from another appropriate National Committee.

MODIFICATION: The Court is to appoint the sole arbitrator or chairman of the tribunal "upon a proposal of a National Committee that it considers to be appropriate" and not "after having requested a proposal from a National Committee that it considers to be appropriate".

COMMENT: The minimal change is designed to accelerate the appointment by the Court of a sole arbitrator or Chairman. Such appointments are made by a Committee of the Court. As modified, Article 9 (3) permits the Secretary General to present to the Committee of the Court not only a suggestion of the National Committee appropriate to propose an arbitrator but also one or more arbitrators proposed by such National Committee. This avoids the delay of the Secretary General suggesting a National Committee to the Committee of the Court and then after the National Committee has been chosen requesting a proposal from that National Committee to be submitted to the Committee of the Court at a future session. Surprisingly, this proposal was considered controversial (Commission meeting of 12, 13 December 1996, ICC Document No. 410/13752), as some National Committees considered that this interfered too much with the absolute discretion of the Court to choose National Committees to make proposals of arbitrators and to confirm such proposals.

It was pointed out that the Court retained its absolute discretion under the proposal and that it was under no obligation to accept the Secretary General's suggestion of the National Committee (a suggestion that the Secretary General also made under the 1975 Rules) or of the specific arbitrators so proposed. The Commission approved the new procedure by a formal vote.

The effect of this modification should be to speed up the arbitral procedure by an estimated 15 to 30 days.

OTHER REFERENCES:

9(4) Where the Court considers that the circumstances so demand, it may choose the sole arbitrator or the chairman of the Arbitral Tribunal from a country where there is no National Committee, provided that neither of the parties objects within the time limit fixed by the Court.

PRIOR TEXT: Second paragraph of Article 2(6), 1975 Rules

Where the Court considers that the circumstances so demand, it may choose the sole arbitrator or the chairman of the arbitral tribunal from a country where there is no National Committee, provided that neither of the parties objects within the time-limit fixed by the Court.

MODIFICATION: Grammatical changes have been made.

COMMENT: The minimal changes that were made were intended to clarify rather than change the provisions set out in the above subsection. The Article was intended to give the court additional flexibility in the nomination of arbitrators. In the past there have been several examples of international arbitrators of renown who were citizens of countries not having National Committees. This Article would permit their appointment by the Court.

OTHER REFERENCES:

9(5) The sole arbitrator or the chairman of the Arbitral Tribunal shall be of a nationality other than those of the parties. However, in suitable circumstances and provided that neither of the parties objects within the time limit fixed by the Court, the sole arbitrator or the chairman of the Arbitral Tribunal may be chosen from a country of which any of the parties is a national.

PRIOR TEXT: The third paragraph of Article 2(6), 1975 Rules

The sole arbitrator or the chairman of the arbitral tribunal shall be chosen from a country other than those of which the parties are nationals. However, in suitable circumstances and provided that neither of the parties objects within the time-limit fixed by the Court, the sole arbitrator or the chairman of the arbitral tribunal may be chosen from a country of which any of the parties is a national.

MODIFICATION: Grammatical changes have been made.

COMMENT: The minimal changes that were made were intended to clarify rather than change the provisions set out in the 1975 Rules. The requirement that, absent agreement by the parties to the contrary, the sole arbitrator or chairman of an arbitral tribunal shall not have the nationality of any of the parties is a key feature of ICC arbitration, of which political neutrality has always been a hallmark. The rules of some international arbitration organizations (such as the LCIA and ICSID) have a similarly strict neutral nationality requirement for the chairman or sole arbitrator appointed by the institution. Others (such as AAA International Rules) do not. ICSID nationality requirements are even more stringent since the Washington Convention's requirements (Article 39) and the method of constituting a three-person tribunal (Rule 3) have as the ordinary result that none of the arbitrators shall have the nationality of a party (unless the parties mutually agree on the appointment of all of the arbitrators).

OTHER REFERENCES:

9(6) Where the Court is to appoint an arbitrator on behalf of a party which has failed to nominate one, it shall make the appointment upon a proposal of the National Committee of the country of which that party is a national. If the Court does not accept the proposal made, or if the National Committee fails to make the proposal requested within the time limit fixed by the Court, or if the country of which the said party is a national has no National Committee, the Court shall be at liberty to choose any person whom it regards as suitable. The Secretariat shall inform the National Committee, if one exists, of the country of which such person is a national.

PRIOR TEXT: Fourth paragraph of Article 2(6), 1975 Rules

Where the Court is to appoint an arbitrator on behalf of a party which has failed to nominate one, it shall make the appointment after having requested a proposal from the National Committee of the country of which the said party is a national. If the Court does not accept the proposal made, or if said National Committee fails to make the proposal requested within the time-limit fixed by the Court, or if the country of which the said party is a national has no National Committee, the Court shall be at liberty to choose any person whom it regards as suitable, after having informed the National Committee of which such person is national, if one exists.

MODIFICATION: Grammatical changes have been made.

COMMENT: The minimal changes that were made were intended to clarify rather than change the provisions set out in the 1975 Rules. In the past, however, the court, having received a recommendation from the Secretariat, would name a National Committee which would then be solicited by the Secretariat to propose an arbitrator. The Secretariat then, sometimes after further discussion with the National Committee, would forward the National Committee's proposal to the Court. The new text (although not very clearly) permits the Secretariat to avoid this two-step process and to solicit a proposal of an arbitrator from an appropriate National Committee and to forward to the Court a recommendation of both the National Committee and the arbitrator. This procedure was approved by the Commission after some discussion and will permit more rapid formation of the arbitral tribunal without in any way diminishing the authority of the Court.

OTHER REFERENCES:

C.P.&P., Section 12.05, "Failure of a party to nominate an arbitrator".

See S. Bond, "The Constitution of the Arbitral Tribunal", *ICC Bull.* Supp. 23 (1997).

Article 10
Multiple Parties

10(1) Where there are multiple parties, whether as Claimant or as Respondent, and where the dispute is to be referred to three arbitrators, the multiple Claimants, jointly, and the multiple Respondents, jointly, shall nominate an arbitrator for confirmation pursuant to Article 9.

PRIOR TEXT: NEW

MODIFICATION: N.A.

COMMENT: The new article sets out the usual method for the appointment of arbitrators for three person ICC Arbitral Tribunals where there are multiple parties. It does not apply where the parties have made a special agreement for the method of appointment of arbitrators, or their number, pursuant to Article 7(6), or where the Court has decided that a sole arbitrator is appropriate. Where there is a three person tribunal the multiple Claimants or multiple Respondents, as the case may be, are invited to name an arbitrator. This has been the prior practice of the Court even though no rule formally set out the procedure. The new article provides a legal underpinning for the prior practice . Where there is no conflict of interest within the group of multiple parties this method of joint appointment causes no particular problem. Usually no conflict arises where related companies forming a group have been joined either as multiple Claimants or as multiple Respondents. Where there are conflicting interests amongst the multiple Claimants or Respondents, problems may arise (*see* Article 10(2)).

While Article 10(1) provides that multiple parties Claimants or Respondents "shall" jointly nominate an arbitrator it might be more correct to state "shall be invited to nominate an arbitrator". This is because Article 10(2) sets out the procedure for what happens when a joint nomination has not been made.

Under the prior practice of the Court, if the multiple Claimants or Respondents failed jointly to name an arbitrator, they would be considered to be in default and the Court would name an arbitrator for the defaulting multiple Claimants or Respondents.

If the other party or parties had nominated an arbitrator, this practice led to a certain disequilibrium among the parties. One party, whether Claimant or Respondent, would have exercised a right to nominate an arbitrator; the adversary multiple Claimants or Respondents, unable to agree jointly on the nomination of an arbitrator, would *see* the appointment made by default by the Court. This problem is now addressed in Article 10(2).

OTHER REFERENCES:

An article with similar intent to the ICC Rules' Article 10 is found in the WIPO Arbitration Rules at Article 18, entitled "Appointment of Three Arbitrators in the

Case of Multiple Claimants or Respondents". The WIPO Rules make a distinction between the cases of multiple Claimants and multiple Respondents.

(a) Where

   i) three arbitrators are to be appointed,

   ii) the parties have not agreed on a procedure of appointment,and

   iii) the Request for Arbitration names more than one Claimant,

the Claimants shall make a joint appointment of an arbitrator in their Request for Arbitration. The appointment of the second arbitrator and the presiding arbitrator shall, subject to paragraph (b) of this Article, take place in accordance with Article 17(b), (c) or (d), as the case may be.

(b) Where

   i) three arbitrators are to be appointed,

   ii) the parties have not agreed on a procedure of appointment, and

   iii) the Request for Arbitration names more than one Respondent,

the Respondents shall jointly appoint an arbitrator. If, for whatever reason, the Respondents do not make a joint appointment of an arbitrator within 30 days after receiving the Request for Arbitration, any appointment of the arbitrator previously made by the Claimant or Claimants shall be considered void and two arbitrators shall be appointed by the Center. The two arbitrators thus appointed shall, within 30 days after the appointment of the second arbitrator, appoint a third arbitrator, who shall be the presiding arbitrator.

(c) Where

   i) three arbitrators are to be appointed,

   ii) the parties have agreed upon a procedure of appointment, and

   iii) the Request for Arbitration names more than one Claimant or more than one Respondent,

paragraphs (a) and (b) of this Article shall, notwithstanding Article 15(a), apply irrespective of any contractual provisions in the Arbitration Agreement with respect to the procedure of appointment, unless those provisions have expressly excluded the application of this Article.

See J.L. Delvolvé, "Report on Multi-Party Arbitrations of the ICC Commission on International Arbitration, 6 *ICC Bull.*, No. 1, 26 (1995).

See "Note from the Secretariat on the Constitution of Arbitral Tribunals in Multi-party cases", 4 *ICC Bull.* 6 (1993).

See Philippe Leboulanger, "Multi-Contract Arbitration", 13 *J. Int'l Arb.* No. 4, p. 43 (1996).

10(2) In the absence of such a joint nomination and where all parties are unable to agree to a method for the constitution of the Arbitral Tribunal, the Court may appoint each member of the Arbitral Tribunal and shall designate one of them to act as chairman. In such case, the Court shall be at liberty to choose any person it regards as suitable to act as arbitrator, applying Article 9 when it considers this appropriate.

PRIOR TEXT: NEW

MODIFICATION: Article 10(2) constitutes an important modification in ICC multi party arbitration practice. In the case of multiple parties Claimant or Respondent (in fact the issue arises almost exclusively in the case of multiple parties Respondent) who were unable or unwilling to agree jointly on an arbitrator (where a three person tribunal was called for) the Court was faced with a dilemma: one alternative would be to choose the arbitrator for the "defaulting" joint parties alone (thus leaving the other party free to choose "its" arbitrator) which would result in a certain inequality in the position of the Claimant and of the Respondent. This was the procedure in prior ICC practice. The other alternative would be for the Court to be given, faced with such a "default" by one group of parties, the power to name all three of the arbitrators. This solution, which preserves the equality, or equilibrium, between the parties, nevertheless deprives one of the parties of the power, which it would wish to exercise, to be able to nominate one of the members of the three person tribunal.

It is the second solution which the revised Rules has now specifically given the Court power to impose.

COMMENT: The solution adopted by the new Rules was inspired in large measure by the *Dutco* case decided by the French Cour de Cassation in January of 1992. *See also* Comment at Article 10(1).

An earlier draft of this modification proposed by the Working Party (ICC Doc. No. 420/15-15 of 8 October 1996) provided that in the absence of the required joint nomination the Court "shall" appoint each member of the Arbitral Tribunal. The adoption of the word "may", consistent with the Court's original proposal, suggests, although it does not clearly so state, that the Court retains discretion to utilize other methods of appointment including the prior practice of naming an arbitrator for the defaulting multiple parties while permitting the other party to nominate its arbitrator. The Court's power to appoint arises only where, after failure of a joint nomination, "all parties are unable to agree to a method for the constitution of the arbitral tribunal". The Secretariat should be consulted in such circumstances, as an agreed method of appointment is encouraged.

There are two reasons why the Rules have retained the right for the Court to insist, in appropriate cases, that multiple parties Claimant or multiple parties Respondent appoint a common arbitrator on default of which the Court would appoint. In the first place, the requirements of the French court in *Dutco* have not been followed in other jurisdictions and the ICC Court should not necessarily feel constrained by that example. In the second place, there are many cases where the multiple parties may have common interests (*i.e.,* parent and subsidiary companies) and it is entirely appropriate in such circumstances to require them to name a common arbitrator.

OTHER REFERENCES: *See also* Other References at Article 10(1).

The Court proposed:

> When multiple parties, whether as Claimants or as Defendants, do not agree on the joint nomination of an arbitrator within the time-limit set by the Court, the Court may appoint the entire arbitral tribunal.

See Cour de Cassation (France) 7 Jan. 1992, 1992 *Rev. arb.* 520; XVIII *Yearbook,* 140 (1993).

The Court ruled in the Dutco case that the principle of equality of the parties in appointing arbitrators is a matter of public policy and can be waived only after the dispute has arisen. Thus, even if the adherence to the 1975 Rules could constitute an agreement before the existence of a dispute by multiple parties to have one arbitrator nominated by the multiple parties, this would not constitute a legally valid waiver of its right to equal treatment where the other party freely nominated an arbitrator. While the Dutco case may continue to inhibit, for arbitrations taking place in France, the naming by the Court of an arbitrator for defaulting multiple parties while permitting the other party to nominate its arbitrator, it has no effect on arbitrations taking place elsewhere.

See E. Schwartz, "Multi-party Arbitration and the ICC in the Wake of Dutco", 10 *J. Int'l Arb.* No. 5, p. 1 (1993) (reprinted in II C.P. & P., International Chamber of Commerce Arbitration, Appendix VI (loose leaf edition)).

See S. Gravel, "Multiparty Arbitration and Multiple Arbitrations", 7 *ICC Bull.,* No. 2, p. 45 (1996).

See Charles Jarrosson, Note on Dutco case, 110 *JDI* (Clunet) 726 (1992).

See ICC Arbitration N° 3879 (Westland Helicopters) interim award of 5 March 1984, XI *Yearbook* 127 (1986). (Contrary to the principles later established in France in the *Dutco* case the Arbitral Tribunal, having Geneva as the place of arbitration, found that it properly had jurisdiction where the ICC Court had appointed one arbitrator for five defendants who had not agreed to make a joint nomination and where the Claimant had nominated an arbitrator. Earlier court proceedings by one of the defendants objecting to the appointment had also been rejected by the Court of Justice of the Court of Geneva).

See C. Seppala, "French Supreme Court Nullifies ICC Practice for Appointment of Arbitrators in Multi-Party Arbitration", 10 *Int'l Construction L. Rev.* 222 (1993).

See S. Bond, "The Constitution of the Arbitral Tribunal", *ICC Bull.* Supp. 23–24 (1997).

Article 11
Challenge of Arbitrators

11(1) A challenge of an arbitrator, whether for an alleged lack of independence or otherwise, shall be made by the submission to the Secretariat of a written statement specifying the facts and circumstances on which the challenge is based.

PRIOR TEXT: First sentence of Article 2(8), 1975 Rules

Article 2(8)

A challenge of an arbitrator, whether for an alleged lack of independence or otherwise, is made by the submission to the Secretary General of the Court of a written statement specifying the facts and circumstances on which the challenge is based.

MODIFICATION: It is now specified that submissions of challenges are to be made to the Secretariat, not to the Secretary General. The Secretariat administers the procedure of challenges which are decided by the Court (*See* Article 11(3)).

COMMENT: For explanation on the new reference to the Secretariat in place of the Secretary General, *see* Article 7(2). Note that while the Rules only specify that an arbitrator shall be "independent" of the parties (Articles 7(1) and 7(2) *supra*) they permit challenges on other grounds. *See* Comment at Article 7(1), *supra*. The most frequent challenges are for financial conflicts of interest (which implicate the financial independence of the arbitrator). However, challenges may also be made for other reasons ("or otherwise") where the arbitrator is not impartial, is biased against a party, or engages in improper conduct. The addition of the words "or otherwise" was made in the 1988 mini-revision to the 1975 Rules.

OTHER REFERENCES:

C.P.&P., Section 13.05, "Grounds for challenge".

See D. Hascher, "ICC Practice in relation to the appointment, confirmation, challenge and replacement of arbitrators", 6 *ICC Bull.* No. 2, 4 (1995).

11(2) For a challenge to be admissible, it must be sent by a party either within 30 days from receipt by that party of the notification of the appointment or confirmation of the arbitrator, or within 30 days from the date when the party making the challenge was informed of the facts and circumstances on which the challenge is based if such date is subsequent to the receipt of such notification.

PRIOR TEXT: Second sentence of Article 2(8), 1975 Rules

For a challenge to be admissible, it must be sent by a party either within 30 days from receipt by that party of the notification of the appointment or confirmation of the arbitrator by the Court; or within 30 days from the date when the party making the challenge was informed of the facts and circumstances on which the challenge is based, if such date is subsequent to the receipt of the aforementioned notification.

MODIFICATION: The explanatory phrase "by the Court" is omitted. *Grammatical changes have been made.*

COMMENT: Should the parties wish to present a challenge of the appointment or confirmation of an arbitrator, this article requires a certain due diligence and timely action if the challenge is to be deemed valid.

OTHER REFERENCES:

C.P.&P., Section 13.08, "Time limits for challenge".

11(3) The Court shall decide on the admissibility, and, at the same time, if necessary, on the merits of a challenge after the Secretariat has afforded an opportunity for the arbitrator concerned, the other party or parties and any other members of the Arbitral Tribunal, to comment in writing within a suitable period of time. Such comments shall be communicated to the parties and to the arbitrators.

PRIOR TEXT: Article 2(9), 1975 Rules

Article 2(9)

The Court shall decide on the admissibility, and at the same time if need be on the merits, of a challenge after the Secretary General of the Court has accorded an opportunity for the arbitrator concerned, the parties and any other members of the arbitral tribunal to comment in writing within a suitable period of time.

MODIFICATION: The reference to the Secretary General is replaced by reference to the Secretariat. The term "the parties" is replaced by "the other party or parties". The word "accorded" is replaced by "afforded". The final proviso is new.

COMMENT: The changes are designed to make the challenge process more transparent. Under prior practice the comments made by the co-arbitrators on a challenge made to another member were not communicated to the parties. Under the new provisions of Article 11(3), the challenge made to the Secretariat is transmitted to the concerned arbitrator, the other arbitrators, and the other party or parties, all of whom may comment thereon to the Secretariat. These comments are now all to be transmitted to the challenging party and this process implicitly gives it the right to comment on the remarks. While the procedure increases transparency and protects the interests of the challenger, it may be suspected that co-arbitrators, knowing that their comments will be released to the parties, will no longer be willing to comment on the comportment or interests of a fellow arbitrator.

OTHER REFERENCES:

C.P. & P. Section 13.06, "Replacement of an arbitrator following resignation, challenge, incapacity, or misconduct".

Article 4(5), 1998 Internal Rules [Appendix II].

Note that the 1998 Internal Rules remove the formal restriction that the three person Committee of the Court may not act on challenges of arbitrators. The Court has decided that questions dealing with the status of an arbitrator (challenge, replacement) will be decided at a Plenary Session. *See* R.Briner, "The Implementation of the 1998 ICC Rules of Arbitration", 8 *ICC Bull.* No. 2, 7, 9 (1997). However, the Court could determine to derogate from this decision of principle in exceptional circumstances.

See S. Bond, "The Constitution of the Arbitral Tribunal", *ICC Bull.* Supp. 22,24 (1997).

Article 12
Replacement of Arbitrators

12(1) An arbitrator shall be replaced upon his death, upon the acceptance by the Court of the arbitrator's resignation, upon acceptance by the Court of a challenge or upon the request of all the parties.

PRIOR TEXT: Article 2(10), 1975 Rules

Article 2(10)

An arbitrator shall be replaced upon his death, upon the acceptance by the court of a challenge, or upon the acceptance by the Court of an arbitrator's resignation.

MODIFICATION: The phrase "or upon the request of all the parties" was added to Article 2(10), 1975 Rules.

COMMENT: The addition of this phrase giving the Court the authority to require an arbitrator to resign upon agreement by all the parties is another instance of reinforcement of the rights of the parties to determine the procedure of the arbitration. Arbitrators should enjoy the confidence of the parties. When all of the parties no longer have such confidence the procedure should provide for reconstitution of the tribunal.

Note that the mere unilateral act of an arbitrator tendering his resignation does not make that resignation effective nor require his replacement. In view of the possibility that a party appointed arbitrator might tender his resignation at the end of the proceedings for the sole purpose of disrupting the proceedings, the Court reserves the right not to accept the resignation, thus requiring the arbitrator to remain in office as an arbitrator.

OTHER REFERENCES:

C.P.&P., Section 13.06, "Replacement of an arbitrator following resignation, challenge, incapacity or misconduct".

See D. Hascher, "ICC practice in relation to the appointment, confirmation, challenge and replacement of arbitrators", 6 *ICC Bull.* No. 2, 4 (1995).

12(2) An arbitrator shall also be replaced on the Court's own initiative when it decides that he is prevented *de jure* or *de facto* from fulfilling his functions, or that he is not fulfilling his functions in accordance with the Rules or within the prescribed time limits.

PRIOR TEXT: First sentence of Article 2(11), 1975 Rules

Article 2(11)

An arbitrator shall also be replaced when the Court decides that he is prevented de jure or de facto from fulfilling his functions, or that he is not fulfilling his functions in accordance with the Rules or within the prescribed time-limits.

MODIFICATION: The phrase "on the Court's own initiative" is added to the first sentence of Article 2(11), 1975 Rules.

COMMENT: The Court has the power to avoid a dysfunctional tribunal by removing an arbitrator who is not fulfilling his duties. The Court's power to remove an arbitrator on its own initiative parallels to a certain extent its power to remove an arbitrator upon challenge of a party under Article 11. At the same time the power is broader as it permits removal for any reason in the interest of justice and to avoid blockage of the arbitral process, including reasons which are not attributable to the fault of the arbitrator. The action would be based on information coming to the Court from the Secretariat based usually on communications to it from the parties or the arbitrators. The power has been used very rarely.

Note that Article 4(5) of the 1998 Internal Rules [Appendix II] removes the formal restriction found in the prior Internal Rules that the power to remove an arbitrator for not fulfilling his functions could not be delegated by the Court to the three-person Committee of the Court. The Court has decided, however, that the issues of replacement of an arbitrator (Article 12(2)), and the procedure for naming a new arbitrator (Article 12 (4)), as well as the possible decision not to replace an arbitrator who has died or been removed subsequent to the closing of proceedings (Article 12 (5)), will be decided in Plenary Session.

OTHER REFERENCES:

C.P.&P., Section 13.07, "Standard of conduct for arbitrators during the proceedings".

See F. Nariman, "Standards of Behavior of Arbitrators", 4 *Arb. Int'l* 311 (1988*)*.

12(3) When, on the basis of information that has come to its attention, the Court considers applying Article 12(2), it shall decide on the matter after the arbitrator concerned, the parties and any other members of the Arbitral Tribunal have had an opportunity to comment in writing within a suitable period of time. Such comments shall be communicated to the parties and to the arbitrators.

PRIOR TEXT: Second sentence of Article 2(11), 1975 Rules

When, on the basis of information that has come to its attention, the Court considers applying the preceding subparagraph, it shall decide on the matter after the Secretary General of the Court has provided such information in writing to the arbitrator concerned, the parties and any other members of the arbitral tribunal, and accorded an opportunity to them to comment in writing within a suitable period of time.

MODIFICATION: The paragraph is modified by omission of the reference to the Secretary General. The requirement that the information coming to the attention of the Court shall be communicated "in writing" to the arbitrator concerned, the parties and any other member of the Tribunal has been eliminated, leaving the Secretariat to communicate the information in any fashion it chooses. The final sentence is new.

COMMENT: It was decided that no formalities need be required before comments are solicited from the arbitrators and the parties on the information that had come to the Court's attention, therefore the clause requiring the Secretary General to "provide such information in writing" is no longer necessary. The normal means of communication, for comment, of the information which would be a basis for replacement would nevertheless be in writing from the Secretariat.

Article 12(3) adopts the same principles of "transparency" as adopted for the challenge procedure in Article 11(3); any comments of parties or co-arbitrators on the failure of an arbitrator to fulfill his functions will be communicated to the parties and the arbitrators.

OTHER REFERENCES:

12(4) When an arbitrator is to be replaced, the Court has discretion to decide whether or not to follow the original nominating process. Once reconstituted, and after having invited the parties to comment, the Arbitral Tribunal shall determine if and to what extent prior proceedings shall be repeated before the reconstituted Arbitral Tribunal.

PRIOR TEXT: Article 2(12), 1975 Rules

Article 2(12)

In each instance where an arbitrator is to be replaced, the procedure indicated in the preceding paragraphs 3, 4, 5 and 6 shall be followed. Once reconstituted, and after having invited the parties to comment, the arbitral tribunal shall determine if and to what extent prior proceedings shall again take place.

MODIFICATION: The phrase "the Court has discretion to decide whether or not to follow the original nominating process" replaces the 1975 Rules' "the procedure indicated in the preceding paragraphs 3, 4, 5 and 6 shall be followed". In the second sentence the Arbitral Tribunal shall determine if and to what extent prior proceedings shall "be repeated before the reconstituted Arbitral Tribunal", rather than "again take place."

COMMENT: Changes have been made for the purposes of clarification.

The provision set out in Article 12(4) allows the Court to sidestep the original nominating process, where appropriate. The reason for giving the Court the power to avoid the usual party nominating procedure to replace a removed arbitrator is that the circumstances calling for replacement may be caused by party conduct leading to the malfunctioning of the tribunal. Permitting the Court to appoint directly a new arbitrator, or to provide for another nominating procedure which also avoids the party appointed arbitrator issue, will, it is hoped, lead to either avoidance or cure of such a problem. This is another instance where the discretionary powers of the Court are reinforced by specific provisions of the 1998 Rules.

The prior provision of the Rules had stated that the reconstituted arbitral tribunal shall decide, in the exercise of its discretion, whether and to what extent prior proceedings must be repeated. Because of the heavy reliance on documentary evidence in ICC arbitration, witness testimony may be considered less important and the necessity to repeat it less essential. On the other hand, where a transcript of prior testimony has not been taken (which is frequently the case in ICC arbitration), this may be considered a factor in requiring testimony to be heard again.

OTHER REFERENCES:

C.P.&P. Section 13.06. "Replacement of an arbitrator following resignation, challenge, incapacity or misconduct".

The Court suggested that the following provision be incorporated into Article 12(3) in order to "preclude the choice by the parties of arbitrators engaging in dilatory tactics":

> However in exceptional circumstances, the Court may replace an arbitrator without requesting a new nomination from a party.

See LCIA Rules, Article 3.5:

> In the event that the Court determined that a nominee is not suitable or independent or impartial, or if an appointed arbitrator is to be replaced, **the Court shall have discretion to decide whether or not to follow the original nominating process**. . . .

12(5) Subsequent to the closing of the proceedings, instead of replacing an arbitrator who has died or been removed by the Court pursuant to Articles 12(1) and 12(2), the Court may decide, when it considers it appropriate, that the remaining arbitrators shall continue the arbitration. In making such determination, the Court shall take into account the views of the remaining arbitrators and of the parties and such other matters that it considers appropriate in the circumstances.

PRIOR TEXT: NEW

MODIFICATIONS: N.A.

COMMENT: The normal procedure following the death or removal by the Court of an arbitrator is the replacement of the arbitrator. Article 12(5) permits the Court, in limited circumstances, to determine that the arbitrator shall not be replaced and that the remaining arbitrators constituting a "truncated tribunal" will continue the proceedings and render a final award. The most important limiting circumstance is that the Court has the power to provide for the continuation of the proceedings by a truncated tribunal only where the death or removal of the arbitrator takes place after the closing of the proceedings (*See* Article 22). In addition the Court will take into account the views of the remaining arbitrators and the parties and the surrounding circumstances before making a determination of the appropriateness of proceeding with a truncated tribunal.

If the death or removal of the arbitrator takes place prior to the closing of the proceedings a replacement must be named. The reason for providing the possibility of a truncated tribunal, albeit in limited circumstances, is to avoid the expense of reconstituting a tribunal which has almost arrived at the end of its mission and where the views of the removed or deceased arbitrator may already be known, while at the same time recognizing that the parties are entitled to have their evidence heard and their case put to a full tribunal. Thus the Court can permit the arbitral tribunal to proceed as a truncated tribunal only after the closure of the proceedings and only after having taken into account the views of the remaining arbitrators and the parties. The Article provides legal justification for permitting the two remaining arbitrators to sign and deliver a final award when one of the arbitrators has died during the period of deliberations (a situation which has arisen on several occasions). It would also be useful in the case where obstructive tactics by a party in collaboration with a party appointed arbitrator led to the latter's removal and to suspicion that the arbitrator's replacement would only lead to more of the same.

The Article does not deal with the situation of what might be called a "limping" tribunal or a *de facto* truncated tribunal where an arbitrator simply fails to participate in the deliberations of the tribunal although duly summoned. In past practice, the Court, without removal of the arbitrator, has sometimes permitted the arbitration to proceed to final award. The non-participating arbitrator will be invited to sign the award and should he refuse, the circumstances of his failure to sign will be stated on the award.

The validity of an award rendered under these conditions may be called into question in some circumstances by some national courts. To determine the appropriate action to take in all the circumstances and whether it is necessary or desirable to resort to the power of Article 12(5), the Court and the Arbitral Tribunal will "act in the spirit of these Rules and shall make every effort to make sure that the award is enforceable at law" as provided in Article 35, the "General Rule".

OTHER REFERENCES:

The WIPO Rules' Article 35 contains a similar provision:

(a) If an arbitrator on a three-person Tribunal, though duly notified and without good cause, fails to participate in the work of the Tribunal, the two other arbitrators shall, unless a party has made an application under Article 32, have the power in their sole discretion to continue the arbitration and to make any award, order or other decision, notwithstanding the failure of the third arbitrator to participate. **In determining whether to continue the arbitration or to render any award, order or other decision without participation of an arbitrator, the two other arbitrators shall take into account the stage of the arbitration, the reason, if any, expressed by the third arbitrator for such non-participation, and such other matters as they consider appropriate in the circumstances of the case.**

The ICC Rules' and the WIPO Rules' provisions set out similar determining factors as to whether or not a case will continue which has only two arbitrators, but while the WIPO Rules leave such discretion to the arbitrators, the ICC Rules reserve such power for the Court itself.

See S.M. Schwebel, "The validity of an arbitral award rendered by a truncated tribunal", 6 *ICC Bull.*, No. 2, p. 19 (1995).

THE ARBITRAL PROCEEDINGS

Article 13
Transmission of the File to the Arbitral Tribunal

The Secretariat shall transmit the file to the Arbitral Tribunal as soon as it has been constituted, provided the advance on costs requested by the Secretariat at this stage has been paid.

PRIOR TEXT: Article 9(3) and Article 10, 1975 Rules

Article 9(3)

The Secretariat may make the transmission of the file to the arbitrator conditional upon the payment by the parties or one of them of the whole or part of the advance on costs to the International Chamber of Commerce.

Article 10

Subject to the provisions of Article 9, the Secretariat shall transmit the file to the arbitrator as soon as it has received the Defendant's answer to the Request for Arbitration, at the latest upon the expiry of the time-limits fixed in Articles 4 and 5 above for the filing of these documents.

MODIFICATION: The conditional phrase, "subject to the provisions of Article 9" is omitted. The file may now be transmitted to the tribunal as soon as the initial advance on costs set by the Secretariat under Article 30(1) has been paid by the Claimant.

COMMENT: These changes are intended to ensure that the arbitral tribunal receive the file as soon as possible. In prior practice there were substantial delays in the fixing of advances on costs to be paid by both parties, and frequent delays in payment by the Respondent. The revision makes it possible for the Claimant alone, and at the outset, to fulfill the conditions for having the file transmitted to the Tribunal by paying the initial advances established for this purpose.   For further comment on the process whereby the Secretary General fixes a provisional advance to be paid by the Claimant, *see* Article 30(2).

OTHER REFERENCES:

The Court recommended that the Article be set out as follows in order to correct a grammatical error:

> Subject to the provisions of Article 9 [advance to court costs], the Secretariat shall transmit the file to the **arbitral tribunal** as soon as it has received the Defendant's Answer to the Request for Arbitration, at the latest upon expiry of the time-limits fixed **pursuant to** Article 4 [Answer to the Request] above for the filing of such document.

Article 14
Place of the Arbitration

14(1) The place of the arbitration shall be fixed by the Court unless agreed upon by the parties.

PRIOR TEXT: Article 12, 1975 Rules

Article 12

Place of Arbitration

The place of arbitration shall be fixed by the International Court of Arbitration, unless agreed upon by the parties.

MODIFICATION: "International Court of Arbitration"is shortened to "Court".

COMMENT: Consideration was given to substituting the word "seat" of the arbitration for "place" to avoid confusion concerning the permanent domiciliation of the Arbitral Tribunal with locations at which certain portions of the arbitral proceedings might take place. Much recent legal writing uses "seat" for just this reason. The Commission decided to retain the phrase "place of arbitration" in view of the fact that this use had not caused any significant problems in the past and that modern arbitration rules in their majority have continued to use "place".

In making this determination, the Court takes into consideration the neutrality (in respect of the parties) of the place of arbitration and the convenience, considering a number of factors, of the location as well as the enforceability of an award rendered there.

OTHER REFERENCE:

C.P.&P., Section 12.01, "Place of arbitration"; *see also* Section 7.02 dealing with the choice of the place of arbitration in the agreement to arbitrate.

LCIA Rules, Article 7 "Place of Arbitration".

AAA Commercial Rules, Article 11 "Fixing of Locale".

AAA International Rules, Article 13 "Place of Arbitration".

UNCITRAL Rules, Article 16 "Place of Arbitration".

WIPO Rules, Article 39 "Place of Arbitration".

Also UNCITRAL Law, Articles 1(3), 20 "Place of Arbitration".

See S. Jarvin, "The Place of Arbitration — A Review of the ICC Court's Guiding Principles and Practice when Fixing the Place of Arbitration", 7 *ICC Bull.*, No. 2, 54 (1996).

See H. Verbist, "The Practice of the ICC International Court of Arbitration With Regard to the Fixing of the Place of Arbitration", 12 *Arb. Int'l* 347 (1996).

14(2) The Arbitral Tribunal may, after consultation with the parties, conduct hearings and meetings at any location it considers appropriate unless otherwise agreed by the parties.

PRIOR TEXT: NEW

MODIFICATION: N.A.

COMMENT: The possibility to conduct hearings or hold meetings at a place other than the official place of arbitration is a convenience which arbitrators and parties have frequently appreciated in the past. In earlier drafts providing for an official "seat" of arbitration it was established that hearings or meetings could be held at other "places". In view of the retention of the official "place" of arbitration (*see* Article 14(1)) it was necessary to provide for meetings at other "locations".

Once a dispute has arisen it is frequently difficult to obtain both parties' agreement on procedural matters, including the place of meetings and hearings. Accordingly, the arbitrators, after consulting the parties, are free to fix a meeting or hearing at a location other than the place of arbitration unless **both** parties do not agree. In most cases, in practice, hearings will be held at the official place of arbitration unless the parties and the arbitrators agree that they should be held elsewhere. The necessity for the arbitrators to consult the parties prior to holding any proceedings outside of the place of arbitration is consistent with the view of the Rules that the proceedings should be conducted according to the agreement of the parties.

The necessity to consult the parties also assuages the concerns of developing countries that if an arbitrator was left completely free in his decisions regarding locales of meetings, he might avoid the intended contact with the described place of arbitration in a developing country.

The recommendation of the Court that it should be given expressly the power to fix another official place of arbitration if exceptional circumstances so require (*see* "Other References" below) was not taken up. The suggestion was based on a few cases that had arisen in recent practice where by reasons of war, changes in legal regime, or otherwise, it had become impossible to hold an ICC arbitration at the designated place. Doubts were expressed as to the legal power of an arbitral institution without the consent of the parties to change the legal status of an arbitration determined by its place. The power of the arbitral tribunal to hold meetings and hearings at other locations should provide an adequate remedy in most cases. In an exceptional case where this was not sufficient to prevent frustration of the arbitral process the Court may retain reserved and discretionary powers to deal with the situation under Article 35, the "General Rule".

OTHER REFERENCES:

The Court recommended that the following provision be added to Article 14 of the 1975 Rules:

> In the event that exceptional circumstances make arbitration impossible at the place so fixed or agreed, the Court may fix another place after consulting the parties.
>
> After consultation of the parties, the arbitrator may decide to hold hearings at any other place.

The Court indicated that "this proposal is necessitated by the prevailing situation in certain countries, the arbitral tribunal remaining free, in any event, to fix the place of hearings. Indeed it is necessary to distinguish between the legal seat of the arbitration, the subject of Article 12 [Article 14] of the Rules, and the different places where the arbitrators and parties may meet for hearings, the taking of evidence, etc".

14(3) The Arbitral Tribunal may deliberate at any location it considers appropriate.

PRIOR TEXT: NEW

MODIFICATIONS: N.A.

COMMENT: Note that the obligation of the arbitrator to consult with the parties prior to holding hearings and meetings at locations other than the official place of arbitration does not apply to meetings and deliberations by the members of the arbitral tribunal themselves. These meetings may be held wherever the members of the arbitral tribunal choose, without obligation to consult the parties or the Secretariat.

Article 15
Rules Governing the Proceedings

15(1) The proceedings before the Arbitral Tribunal shall be governed by these Rules, and where these Rules are silent, by any rules which the parties or, failing them, the Arbitral Tribunal, may settle on, whether or not reference is thereby made to the rules of procedure of a national law to be applied to the arbitration.

PRIOR TEXT: Article 11, 1975 Rules

Article 11

Rules governing the proceedings

The rules governing the proceedings before the arbitrator shall be those resulting from these Rules and, where these Rules are silent, any rules which the parties (or failing them, the arbitrator) may settle, and whether or not reference is thereby made to a municipal procedural law to be applied to the arbitration.

MODIFICATION: "[T]he rules of procedure of a national law" replaces "municipal procedural law".

COMMENT: The change from "municipal" procedural law to "the rules of procedure of a national law" is not intended to make any substantive change. The reference to municipal law was always intended to refer to national law as contrasted with international law and reflecting the somewhat old fashioned academic divisions of international law and municipal law. Since some people confused this reference to municipal law as a law regulating cities or municipalities, the clarifying change was made. Some National Committees, in their comments to the Commission on the new draft, had some reservations as to whether the new wording might cause some confusion in countries having a federal system of government — federal or national law on the one hand and state law on the other. It is clear from the context that "the rules of procedure of national law" refers to the applicable procedural laws of any nation or its subdivisions.

OTHER REFERENCES:

C.P.&P., Chapter 16, "Rules Governing the Proceedings".

15(2) In all cases, the Arbitral Tribunal shall act fairly and impartially and ensure that each party has a reasonable opportunity to present its case.

PRIOR TEXT: NEW

MODIFICATION: N.A.

COMMENT: This addition may seem to be surplusage: fairness and equality are fundamental to and implicit conditions of arbitration procedure. They have always been required in ICC arbitration practice. Following the lead of more recent arbitration rules, however, it was thought advisable to make these conditions explicit.

The choice of the term "reasonable opportunity to present its case" as opposed to the "full opportunity" set out in the UNCITRAL Rules was purposeful. A disappointed party may always believe that it should have still another opportunity to present its case, bring in new evidence or make reargument. The Arbitral Tribunal has full discretion to determine what is reasonable in the circumstances.

OTHER REFERENCES:

See ICC Rules, Article 7(1) ("independence" of the arbitrator), Article 11 (possibility to challenge an arbitrator "whether for lack of independence or otherwise").

AAA International Rules, Article 16 "Conduct of the Arbitration"

> 1. Subject to these rules, the tribunal may conduct the arbitration in whatever manner it considers appropriate, provided that the parties are treated with equality and that each party has the right to be heard and is given a fair opportunity to present its case.

UNCITRAL Rules, Article 15 " Arbitral proceedings, General Provisions"

> 1. Subject to these Rules, the arbitral tribunal may conduct the arbitration in such manner as it considers appropriate, provided that the parties are treated with equality and that at any stage of the proceedings each party is given a full opportunity of presenting his case.

WIPO Rules, Article 38, "General Powers of the Tribunal"

> (a) Subject to Article 3, the Tribunal may conduct the arbitration in such manner as it considers appropriate.

> (b) In all cases, the Tribunal shall ensure that the parties are treated with equality and that each party is given a fair opportunity to present its case.

The requirement that an arbitrator shall act fairly and impartially is also considered to be an ethical obligation. *See* IBA Rules of Ethics for International Arbitrators. Article 1 provides that an arbitrator "shall be and shall remain free of bias" and Article 3 provides that "[t]he criteria for assessing questions relating to bias are impartiality and independence".

Article 16
Language of the Arbitration

16(1) In the absence of an agreement by the parties, the Arbitral Tribunal shall determine the language or languages of the arbitration, due regard being given to all relevant circumstances, including the language of the contract.

PRIOR TEXT: Article 15(3), 1975 Rules

Article 15(3)

The arbitrator shall determine the language or languages of the arbitration, due regard being paid to all the relevant circumstances and in particular to the language of the contract.

MODIFICATION:

> In the absence of an agreement by the parties" has been inserted before the text of Article 15(3), 1975 Rules to make clear that the parties may in the arbitration agreement, or subsequently, determine the language (or languages) in which the arbitration will be conducted. In fact, parties more and more frequently set out in the arbitration clause the language of the arbitration. The addition of the conditional phrase "In the absence of an agreement by the parties. . . " encourages the parties to fix the language of the arbitration in the arbitration clause decided between them.

> Where the tribunal must decide the language of the arbitration it is provided in the new Rules that it will take into account "all relevant circumstances including the language of the contract" and not, as before "all the relevant circumstances and in particular to the language of the contract.

COMMENT: The change in text was suggested by the French National Committee and was adopted by a closely contested vote at the meeting of the Commission on International Arbitration of 27 February 1997. The new text gives more discretion to the arbitral tribunal to take into account factors other than the language of the contract and reflects a reaction of French speaking national committees to what they see as too automatic an adoption of English as the language of the arbitration (based on English language contract documents) when factors such as the languages of the parties and their counsel might suggest another more appropriate choice.

The new rule may also be useful in dealing with contracts with states or state emanations in which by reason of the law or constitution of the state the binding version of the contract is in the state's language, although the negotiated version of the contract and all works thereunder take place under another language (usually English, but on occasion French, Spanish or another common language). In ICC arbitration practice there has almost always been agreement between the parties that the arbitration will take place in the commonly used language and not in the official language. The rule modification reinforces the Arbitral Tribunal's discretion in the matter should problems arise in the future.

It would be reasonable to predict that the effect of the modification of the Article on the choice of the language of the arbitration will be slight in view of the substantial discretion which the Arbitral Tribunal had under the prior text's language and which has now been reinforced.

OTHER REFERENCES:

C.P.&P., Section 7.03, "Language of Arbitration".

See ICC Arb. No. 6228 of 1990, 8 *ICC Bull.* No. 1.53 (1997) (although the language of the arbitration was English, a Request for Arbitration filed in French, and subsequently translated, constituted a valid initiation of arbitration).

See S. Lazareff, "The Language of Institutional Arbitration", 8 *ICC Bull.* No. 1, 18 (1997).

Article 17
Applicable Rules of Law

17(1) The parties shall be free to agree upon the rules of law to be applied by the Arbitral Tribunal to the merits of the dispute. In the absence of any such agreement, the Arbitral Tribunal shall apply the rules of law which it determines to be appropriate.

PRIOR TEXT: Article 13(3), 1975 Rules

Article 13(3)

The parties shall be free to determine the law to be applied by the arbitrator to the merits of the dispute. In the absence of any indication by the parties as to the applicable law, the arbitrator shall apply the law designated as the proper law by the rule of conflict he deems appropriate.

MODIFICATION: In the first sentence it is made clear that parties may choose the application of "rules of law" which is a broader standard than the prior "the law". The second sentence gives the power to the Arbitral Tribunal, in the absence of an agreement by the parties, to apply "rules of law" and not only "the law" which it replaces. The obligation for the arbitrator to apply the law "designated as the proper law by the rules of conflict he deems appropriate" has been dropped. "Arbitral Tribunal" replaces "arbitrator" and "arbitrators".

COMMENT: The modification of the Rules confirms the liberal power of the parties to determine the legal standards governing their obligations. While most contracts provide for the application of a single national law, parties sometimes choose independent rules of law such as the Vienna Sales Convention, or the UNIDROIT Principles of International Commercial Contracts, or "the rules of law governing contractual obligations common to England and France". Parties may also choose to apply "general principles of international law" or similar formulations (such as the principles of *lex mercatoria*), although it should be recognized that such formulations seldom supply sufficiently defined standards to resolve all the legal issues which may arise. The revised Rules confirm that when parties act in this way arbitrators should accept their decision.

When the parties have not made any determination, Article 17(1) gives to the Arbitral Tribunal the power to apply "rules of law", thus a broader power than that granted by Article 13(3) of the 1975 Rules which implies a requirement to choose a single national law, which is to be the "proper law" of the contract as designated by a rule of conflicts of law, a requirement which was not respected in prior arbitral practices in any event.

Even if in most cases where the parties have not designated the applicable rules of law it may be expected that the Arbitral Tribunal will choose a single national law as governing the obligations of the parties, Article 17(1) gives the Arbitral Tribunal a wider freedom in these circumstances than it theoretically enjoyed under the prior Rules. The Arbitral Tribunal is free to apply directly the law which it deems appropriate without any necessity to investigate any "rule of conflict", whether of a national law or otherwise, in making that determination. This empowerment to use the "*voie directe*" in choice of law also coincides with the tendencies of recent arbitral practice.

The freedom of the Arbitral Tribunal, like that of the parties, to apply rules of law other than those of a single state, provides a flexibility which may be helpful to meet the intentions of the parties and to respond to all the circumstances of a case.

OTHER REFERENCES:

C.P.&P., Chapter 17, "Choice of Substantive Law".

See Y. Derains, "The ICC Arbitral Process, Part VIII: Choice of the Law Applicable to the Contract and International Arbitration", 6 *ICC Bull.* No. 1, 10 (1995).

See M. Blessing, "Keynotes on Arbitral Decision Making", *ICC Bull.* Supp. 44, 46-49 (1997).

See M. Blessing, "Choice of Substantive Law in Arbitration", 14 *J. Int'l Arb.* No. 7, 399-446 (1997).

17(2) In all cases, the Arbitral Tribunal shall take account of the provisions of the contract and the relevant trade usages.

PRIOR TEXT: Article 13(5), 1975 Rules

Article 13(5)

In all cases, the arbitrator shall take account of the provisions of the contract and of the relevant trade usages.

MODIFICATION: "Arbitrator" is replaced by "Arbitral Tribunal".

COMMENT: N.A.

OTHER REFERENCES:

C.P. & P., Section 17.03, "Application of contractual terms, relevant trade usage and "*lex mercatoria*".

See Y. Derains, "Le statut des usages du commerce international devant les juridictions arbitrales", 1973 *Rev. arb.* 132.

See P. Fouchard, "Les usages l'arbitre et le juge" in *Le droit des relations economiques internationales* 361 (Liber amicorum for Berthold Goldman) (1982).

See Dossiers of the Institute, "International Trade Usage", ICC Pub. No. 440/4.

17(3) The Arbitral Tribunal shall assume the powers of an *amiable compositeur* or decide *ex aequo et bono* only if the parties have agreed to give it such powers.

PRIOR TEXT: Article 13(4), 1975 Rules

"The arbitrator shall assume the powers of an amiable compositeur if the parties are agreed to give him such powers."

MODIFICATION: The phrase "or decide *ex aequo et bono* only" is added.

COMMENT: The term *"ex aequo et bono"* adopted in this subsection is used by the UNCITRAL Rules as well as some other institutional rules. There is some dispute as to whether the powers of an Arbitral Tribunal acting as *amiable compositeur* or *ex aequo et bono* are coextensive or somewhat differing, a question which may depend on the law in effect at the place of arbitration. Both regimes give broader powers to an arbitrator than those permitted in an arbitration at law and should only be exercised if the parties have specifically so agreed. Since ICC arbitration clauses from time to time refer to *ex aequo et bono* arbitration it was thought prudent to specifically provide for these powers in addition to those of an amiable compositeur where the parties had so agreed.

OTHER REFERENCES:

UNCITRAL Rules, Article 33(2)

> **The arbitral tribunal shall decide as *amiable compositeur* or *ex aequo et bono*** only if the parties have expressly authorized the arbitral tribunal to do so and if the law applicable to the arbitral procedure permits such arbitration.

C.P.&P., Section 18.02, "'Amiable Composition' under the ICC Rules".

See M. Rubino-Sammartano, *"Amiable Compositeur* (Joint Mandate to Settle) and *Ex Bono et Aequo* (Discretional Authority to Mitigate Strict Law) — Apparent Synonyms Revisited", 9 *J. Int'l. Arb.* No. 1, p. 5 (1992).

Article 18
Terms of Reference; Procedural Timetable

18(1) As soon as it has received the file from the Secretariat, the Arbitral Tribunal shall draw up, on the basis of documents or in the presence of the parties and in the light of their most recent submissions, a document defining its Terms of Reference. This document shall include the following particulars :

a) the full names and descriptions of the parties;

b) the addresses of the parties to which notifications and communications arising in the course of the arbitration may be made;

c) a summary of the parties' respective claims and of the relief sought by each party, with an indication to the extent possible of the amounts claimed or counterclaimed;

d) unless the Arbitral Tribunal considers it inappropriate, a list of issues to be determined;

e) the full names, descriptions and addresses of the arbitrators;

f) the place of the arbitration; and

g) particulars of the applicable procedural rules and, if such is the case, reference to the power conferred upon the Arbitral Tribunal to act as *amiable compositeur* **or to decide** *ex aequo et bono.*

PRIOR TEXT: Article 13(1), 1975 Rules

Article 13

Terms of Reference

(1) Before proceeding with the preparation of the case, the arbitrator shall draw up, on the basis of the documents or in the presence of the parties and in the light of their most recent submissions, a document defining its Terms of Reference. This document shall include the following particulars:

a) the full names and description of the parties,

b) the addresses of the parties to which notifications and communications arising in the course of the arbitration may validly be made,

c) a summary of the parties' respective claims,

d) definition of the issues to be determined,

e) the arbitrator's full name, description and address of the arbitrators,

f) the place of arbitration,

g) *particulars of the applicable procedural rules and, if such is the case, reference to the power conferred upon the arbitrator to act as amiable compositeur,*

h) *such other particulars as may be required to make the arbitral award enforceable in law, or may be regarded as helpful by the International Court of Arbitration or the arbitrator.*

MODIFICATION: "Before proceeding with the preparation of the case" is replaced by "As soon as it has received the file from the Secretariat";

a) "Description" is made plural;

b) the term "validly" is omitted;

c) the requirement that relief sought by the parties as well as amounts claimed or counterclaimed be included in the Terms of Reference is added;

d) the phrase "unless an Arbitral Tribunal considers it inappropriate" is added to the requirement of the 1975 rules that the Terms contain "a definition of the issue to be determined";

e) the phrase is inverted;

f) unmodified;

g) the phrase ". . . or to decide *ex aequo et bono*" is added.

Paragraph "h" of prior Article 13 as set out above has been eliminated. The Working Party found that it was unnecessary since "it meets no practical need and is generally ignored by the parties".

COMMENT: Drawing up Terms of Reference remains one of the key characteristics of ICC arbitration. Suggestions to eliminate the Terms or make them optional, in the interest of expediting the arbitral process, were rejected by the Working Party and the Arbitration Commission after consultation with the National Committees which by a large majority supported their retention

However, one important characteristic of the Rules—the necessity for the Arbitral Tribunal to set out a list of issues to be decided—has been attenuated as Article 13(d) of the 1998 Rules provides that the Terms shall provide such a list "unless the Arbitral Tribunal considers it inappropriate". The question of whether the Arbitral Tribunal should be required to list issues in the Terms was discussed at length by the Working Party. Some National Committee had questioned, based on practice, whether the issues involved in the dispute can be known, and described, at an early stage of the proceedings when the Terms are drawn up.

This concern is all the more true under the 1998 Rules since the requirement for alleging in the Request a full statement of the Claimant's case has been somewhat relaxed (*see* Article 4(b)(3), and commentary thereunder). Issues, in any event, tend to evolve with the case. Those new issues not included in the list required in the Terms of Reference are not excluded from consideration in any event. Why not, it was argued, leave the necessity of a list of issues to be determined to the discretion of the arbitrator, as defining the issues may delay the arbitration?

In fact, under the 1975 Rules, which required a description of the issues to be set out in the Terms of Reference, a significant number of arbitrators had routinely avoided the requirement by utilizing a generic formula such as "The issues to be determined by the arbitrators will be those contained in the parties' pleadings and such other issues as may arise during the course of the arbitration". The Court did not object to such formulae when the terms were transmitted to it.

The 1998 Rules give the Arbitral Tribunal discretion to go beyond this tolerated generic description of issues and to abandon any listing at all if it determines such listing to be inappropriate. Nevertheless, the provision that in ordinary cases the Terms shall contain a listing of issues, reflects the ICC's recognition that the Terms remains an essential part of ICC arbitration and the desire that they be as meaningful as possible. This is made clear by the fact that (as set out in the Overview *supra*,) the wording of Article 18(1)d as finally adopted by the Council of the ICC in its April 1997 meeting in Shangai is stronger than the recommendation of the Working Party as confirmed by the Commission at its meeting of 27 February 1997 that a list of issues be containded in the Terms only "if the Arbitral Tribunal considers it appropriate".

In the final version the presumption has been reversed and the listing of issues should be considered the norm. In both cases the giving of discretion to the Tribunal not to list issues was motivated as a compromise to those who advocated making optional the Terms of Reference and to respond to criticisms concerning the delays which attempts to draft an acceptable list of issues could cause in some cases.

OTHER REFERENCES:

C.P.&P., Chapter 15, "Terms of Reference".

See S. Lazareff, "Terms of Reference - A Practical Guide", 3 *ICC Bull.* No. 1, p. 24 (1992), reprinted in II. C.P.&P. Appendix V (looseleaf edition) (A comprehensive guide prepared by an ICC Arbitration Commission Working Party, this reference gives many useful recommendations for arbitrators).

See A. Reiner, "Terms of Reference: The Function of the International Court of *Arbi*tration and Application of Article 16 [Article 18] by the Arbitrator", 7 *ICC Bull.*, No. 2 (1996).

See E. Shafer, "ICC Arbitral Process, Pt. II: Terms of Reference in the Past and at Present", 3 *ICC Bull.*, No. 1.

See J.J. Arnaldez, "L'acte déterminant la mission de l'arbitre" in *Études Offertes à Pierre Bellet*, Paris, Litec, (1991).

See Société Farhat Trading Co. v. Société Daewoo, Cass. Civ. 6 March 1996, 1997 *Rev. arb.* 69, note J.J. Arnaldez (the extent of the arbitrator's jurisdiction is determined by the terms of the arbitration agreement. Within the scope of that jurisdiction the arbitrator may decide all issues which have been properly raised by the claims of the parties. The arbitrator is not limited to deciding only the issues set out in the Terms of Reference).

See M. Schneider, "The Terms of Reference", *ICC Bull.* Supp. 26, 29 (1997). In his article, Mr. Schneider suggests that: "In all cases where a list is included in the Terms of Reference, it should contain a general item that permits the Arbitral Tribunal to complete it as will be required in the light of the latest submission of the parties. It should also be stated clearly in the Terms of Reference that the Arbitral Tribunal is not required to decide all issues on the list, if, in its view, this is not necessary for the award". The Lazareff Report, *supra*, provides the following model for insertion in the Terms: "The issues to be determined shall be those resulting from the parties' submissions and which are relevant to adjudication of the parties' respective claims and defenses. In particular, the Arbitral Tribunal may have to consider the following issues (not necessarily all of these and only these, and not in the following order . . .)".

18(2) The Terms of Reference shall be signed by the parties and the Arbitral Tribunal. Within two months of the date on which the file has been transmitted to it, the Arbitral Tribunal shall transmit to the Court the Terms of Reference signed by it and by the parties. The Court may extend this time limit pursuant to a reasoned request from the Arbitral Tribunal or on its own initiative, if it decides it is necessary to do so.

PRIOR TEXT: First 3 sentences of Article 13(2), 1975 Rules

The document mentioned in paragraph 1 of this Article shall be signed by the parties and the arbitrator. Within two months of the date when the file has been transmitted to him, the arbitrator shall transmit to the Court the said document signed by himself and by the parties. The Court may, pursuant to a reasoned request from the arbitrator or if need be on its own initiative, extend this time-limit if it decides it is necessary to do so.

MODIFICATION: "Terms of Reference" is used in place of "the document mentioned. . . " and "such document". The term "arbitrator" is replaced by "Arbitral Tribunal".

COMMENT: It is a not infrequent occurrence that for perfectly understandable reasons (including the desire to schedule a Terms of Reference meeting which may be complicated by the distance of parties from the place of arbitration or, where no meeting is scheduled, the delays occasioned by communication of draft Terms to the parties and multiple suggested revisions) the Terms cannot be finalized and signed within the two month period. Extensions of the two month period are granted by the Court.

OTHER REFERENCES:

The Court recommended that the following sentence be added to the end of 18(2), in order to provide greater flexibility in the administration of the arbitration:

> In the same manner, the Court may decide to extend any other time-limit fixed by the parties.

C.P.&P., Chapter 15, "Terms of Reference", Section 15.04 "Entry into Effect".

18(3) If any of the parties refuses to take part in the drawing up of the Terms of Reference or to sign the same, they shall be submitted to the Court for approval. When the Terms of Reference are signed in accordance with Article 18(2) or approved by the Court, the arbitration shall proceed.

PRIOR TEXT: Last two sentences of Article 13(2), 1975 Rules

Should one of the parties refuse to take part in the drawing up of the said document or to sign the same, the Court, if it is satisfied that the case is one of those mentioned in paragraphs 2 and 3 of Article 8, shall take such action as is necessary for its approval. Thereafter the Court shall set a time-limit for the signature by the defaulting party and on expiry of that time-limit the arbitration shall proceed and the award shall be made.

MODIFICATION: The second phrase of the first sentence one referring to paragraphs 2 and 3 of Article 8 (of the 1975 Rules) is omitted, and "they shall be submitted to the Court for approval" replaces "shall take such action as is necessary for its approval". The second sentence of the 1998 Rules is simplified, and the requirement of giving to the defaulting party a new time limit for signing the Terms has been eliminated, and a reference to Article 18(2) has been added.

COMMENT: Article 8(2) and 8(3) of the 1975 Rules dealt with the specific cases where a party refuses or fails to take part in the arbitration, or contests the validity or existence of the arbitration agreement. However, there are numerous other situations when a party may refuse to sign the Terms (*e.g.* disagreement with the issues formulated by the Tribunal or other items set out in the Terms). The reference in Article 13(2) of the 1975 Rules to those paragraphs implied that the power of the Court to approve Terms not signed by a party was limited to cases where the party's refusal to sign was motivated by the specified reasons. This was neither the intent of the prior article nor the result in prior practice. The revision makes this clear.

The second sentence has been modified to ensure that an arbitration should proceed immediately after approval by the Court of the Terms of Reference following a default in signature. It was determined that no further time limits for the defaulting party were necessary. This is another example of efforts made in the revision of the Rules to accelerate the arbitral procedure and reduce opportunities for a party to use delaying tactics.

OTHER REFERENCES:

C.P.&P., Section 15.03, "Default by Party".

18(4) When drawing up the Terms of Reference, or as soon as possible thereafter, the Arbitral Tribunal, after having consulted the parties, shall establish in a separate document a provisional timetable that it intends to follow for the conduct of the arbitration and shall communicate it to the Court and the parties. Any subsequent modifications of the provisional timetable shall be communicated to the Court and the parties.

PRIOR TEXT: NEW

MODIFICATIONS: N.A.

COMMENT: With the addition of this subsection to Article 18, the Rules require the Arbitral Tribunal to set up a timetable for the arbitration. In the past, the ICC Court has been accused of extending time limits rather than managing them, thus it was felt that a timetable would create guidelines for the arbitrators and, at the same time, respond to criticism of the excessive length of some arbitration proceedings. The timetable is expressly stated to be "provisional" in order not to create deadlines which may be, in some cases, impossible to meet; an inflexible time-table required by the Rules would threaten the integrity of the arbitral process. For the same reason, it is provided that the timetable is to be established in a separate document established by the Arbitral Tribunal and not in the Terms themselves, which will be signed by the parties. This is to avoid any implication that the timetable has become part of the arbitration agreement or of the procedures agreed to by the parties and that any departure from the agreement could lead to the nullity of an award.

OTHER REFERENCES:

See S. Bruna, "Control of Time Limits by the International Court of Arbitration", 7 *ICC Bull.*, No. 2 (1996).

Article 19
New Claims

After the Terms of Reference have been signed or approved by the Court, no party shall make new claims or counter claims which fall outside the limits of the Terms of Reference unless it has been authorized to do so by the Arbitral Tribunal, which shall consider the nature of such new claims or counterclaims, the stage of the arbitration and other relevant circumstances.

PRIOR TEXT: Article 16, 1975 Rules

Article 16

The parties may make new claims or counter-claims before the arbitrator on condition that these remain within the limits fixed by the Terms of Reference provided for in Article 13 or that they are specified in a rider to that document, signed by the parties and communicated to the International Court of Arbitration.

MODIFICATION: The provision of Article 16 of the 1975 Rules that "parties may make new claims or counterclaims before the arbitrator on condition that these claims remain within the limits fixed by the Terms of Reference" is carried over into the new Rules, although phrased in the negative: ". . . no party shall make new claims or counterclaims which fall outside the limits of the Terms of Reference. . . ". The innovation of the new Article 19 is that the parties may make new claims or counterclaims outside the limits of the Terms if ". . . it has been authorized to do so by the Arbitral Tribunal. . . ". Under the 1975 Rules such a claim or counterclaim outside the limits fixed by the Terms could only be made if the other party or parties to the arbitration agreed and a rider to the Terms, signed by all parties and the arbitrators, was communicated to the Court.

COMMENT: The new provision gives more power and flexibility to the Arbitral Tribunal in dealing with the problem of new claims and counterclaims which are connected with the agreement and dispute spelled out in the Terms but which were not made prior to the signature of that document. In practice, the rigidity of the old Rules had permitted one of the parties, as a dilatory tactic, to prevent an arbitral tribunal from considering a claim or counterclaims which for all reasons of economy and equitable treatment should have been considered with the others but which had been tardily identified or raised. The new Rules permit the Arbitral Tribunal to take into account all appropriate circumstances before ruling on whether to admit a new claim or counterclaim.

It should be stressed that the further elaboration of claims or counterclaims which were within the limits of the Terms may be made freely by the parties, without the necessity of seeking the approval of the Arbitral Tribunal. Moreover as in the past, the restraint or prohibition of raising new claims or counterclaims does not affect the power of the parties to raise new issues or defenses not contained in the Terms.

OTHER REFERENCES:

C.P.&P., Section 15.02, "Terms of Reference: Contents".

See ICC Award No. 3267 of 28 March 1994, 12 *Yearbook* 87 (1987). (The Arbitral Tribunal determined that new claims, beyond the scope of the Terms of Reference, filed at the end of the proceedings were outside the jurisdiction of the Tribunal and could not be adjudicated by it).

See P. Level, "Joinder of Proceedings, Intervention of Third Parties, and Additional Claims and Counterclaims", 7 *ICC Bull.* No. 2, 36 (1996).

See A. Reiner, "Terms of Reference: the Function of the ICA and Application of Article 16 by the Arbitrators", 7 *ICC Bull.* No. 2, 59 (1996).

See ICC Arbitration No. 7076 of 1993; *ICC Bull.* No. 1, 66 (increase of quantification of claim or counterclaim subsequent to signature of Terms of Reference does not constitute a new claim or counterclaim, citing C.P.&P., at p. 255).

For a case finding that the adding of a claim of consequential damages after signature of the Terms of Reference, and the granting of an award thereon did not violate the Rules, *see* Carte Blanche (Singapore) v. Carte Blanche International, Ltd., 683 F. Supp. 945 (S.D.N.Y. 1988).

Article 20
Establishing the Facts of the Case

20(1) The Arbitral Tribunal shall proceed within as short a time as possible to establish the facts of the case by all appropriate means.

PRIOR TEXT: First sentence of article 14(1)

The Arbitral proceedings

The arbitrator shall proceed within as short a time as possible to establish the facts of the case by all appropriate means.

MODIFICATION: The word "Arbitral Tribunal" replaces "arbitrator".

COMMENT: Many other institutional arbitration rules provide in some detail how evidence will be taken and witnesses heard in establishing the facts of the case. The revision of the Rules does not adopt this course, one of the desiderata of the revision being that the basic structure and simplicity of the Rules was to be retained.

OTHER REFERENCES:

C.P. & P., Sec. 23.01, "Arbitrator's power to establish facts by all appropriate means".

See Dossiers of the Institute, "The Taking of Evidence in the Arbitral Proceedings", ICC Pub. No. 440/8.

See M. Blessing, "The Procedure Before the Arbitral Tribunal", 3 *ICC Bull.* No. 2, 18 (1992).

20(2) After studying the written submissions of the parties and all documents relied upon, the Arbitral Tribunal shall hear the parties together in person if any of them so requests or, failing such a request, it may of its own motion decide to hear them.

PRIOR TEXT: Second sentence of Article 14(1)

After study of the written submissions of the parties and of all documents relied upon, the arbitrator shall hear the parties together in person if one of them so requests, and failing such a request he may of his own motion decide to hear them.

MODIFICATION: Grammatical changes have been made.

COMMENT: The right of a party (or, in the case of a corporation, the representative of a party) to be heard is essential and continues to be protected by this provision without changes; while the arbitral tribunal may theoretically refuse to hear witnesses, and may certainly limit their number, the parties must be heard. Whether the party in giving his statement or testimony is to be considered as a witness, or as having a different capacity, is not settled in the Rules and may depend on the legal tradition of the parties and of the arbitrators, the place of arbitration, and other factors.

OTHER REFERENCES:

C.P. & P., Sec. 25.02 "Testimony" (Distinction between witnesses and party representatives).

See ICC Arbitration No. 7319, Procedural Order of 30 October 1992, 1994 *JDI* 1102 (the Arbitral Tribunal considered the Directors of a corporation to be its legal representatives, who would be heard as the "party", not as witnesses, while employees of the corporation were heard as witnesses).

20(3) The Arbitral Tribunal may decide to hear witnesses, experts appointed by the parties or any other person, in the presence of the parties, or in their absence provided they have been duly summoned.

PRIOR TEXT: Third sentence of Article 14(1)

In addition, the arbitrator may decide to hear any other person in the presence of the parties or in their absence provided they have been duly summoned.

MODIFICATION: The term "Arbitral Tribunal" is used in place of "arbitrator". The phrase "witnesses, experts appointed by the parties, or" is added.

COMMENT: The addition of the express provision that the Arbitral Tribunal may hear "experts appointed by the parties" confirms present practice. A party-appointed expert was certainly an "other person" who could be heard as a witness as provided under the 1975 Rules. The purpose of the addition is simply to make the possibility clear and to respond to any semantic arguments that the testimony of an expert is not that of a witness because he does not testify to his own knowledge about any facts contemporaneous to the dispute.

By use of the word "may" the Article confirms, as in the past, that the Arbitral Tribunal has broad discretion as to how it organizes hearings. For its discretionary power not to hear witnesses *see* Comment under Article 20(2).

OTHER REFERENCES:

C.P. & P., Sec. 25.03 "Party experts".

See ICC Arbitration No. 4815, Procedural Order of 9 June 1987, 1996 *JDI* 1042, note D.H. (In an arbitration under the 1975 Rules the Tribunal named a neutral expert and provided by procedural order for the hearing of witnesses of fact but, somewhat unusually, excluded the hearing of party expert witnesses).

See ICC Arbitration No. 1512, Dalmia Dairy Industries, Ltd. (India) v. National Bank of Pakistan, 1 *Yearbook* 128 (1976), V *Yearbook* 170 and 174 (1980) (refusal of sole arbitrator to hear offered witness testimony as not relevant or necessary; sustained on appeal [1978] 2 *Lloyd's L. Rep.* 223 (England), *see also* comment in C.P.&P., Sec. 23.01).

See ICC Arbitration No. 7170, Procedural Order of 15 November 1991, 1993 *JDI* 1062, note D.H. (An arbitral tribunal is not required to hear witnesses. If witnesses are to be heard, the tribunal should assure that a list of the witnesses to be heard and the subject of their proposed testimony is communicated in advance to the tribunal and the other party).

See Dossiers of the Institute, "Arbitration and Expertise", ICC Pub. No. 480/7 (1994).

See Dossiers of the Institute, "The Taking of Evidence in the Arbitral Proceedings", ICC Pub. No. 440/8.

See generally, M. Schneider, 1993 *Swiss Bull.* No. 2, 302, "Witnesses in international arbitration, presentation of materials from arbitration practice".

20(4) The Arbitral Tribunal, after having consulted the parties, may appoint one or more experts, define their terms of reference and receive their reports. At the request of a party, the parties shall be given the opportunity to question at a hearing any such expert appointed by the Tribunal.

PRIOR TEXT: Article 14(2), 1975 Rules

Article 14(2)

The arbitrator may appoint one or more experts, define their Terms of Reference, receive their reports and/or hear them in person.

MODIFICATION: The term "arbitrator" is replaced by "Arbitral Tribunal". The sentences have been reorganized, and reference to the opportunity given to the parties "to question at a hearing any such expert appointed by the Tribunal" is added.

COMMENT: This Article deals with neutral tribunal-appointed experts as opposed to party-named experts. If an expert were appointed by the Tribunal and rendered a report to it without the parties having the right to question the expert, the parties' rights to be heard would be jeopardized. By specifying that any party who requests it shall be given the right to question an expert who has rendered a report, the 1998 Rules make explicit what had been usual ICC arbitral practice.

OTHER REFERENCES:

C.P.&P., Sec. 26.04, "Experts appointed by the Tribunal".

See ICC Arbitration No. 5715, Procedural Order of 28 February 1989, 1996 *JDI* 1050 (Appointment of two experts by Tribunal which defined their mission and assured respect of the principles of confidentiality and procedural due process).

See ICC Arbitration No. 6057, Procedural Order made in 1990, 1993 *JDI* 1068 (usual terms for appointment of technical expert, advance on costs of the expert to be made by the parties).

See Dossiers of the Institute, Arbitration and Expertise, ICC Publication No. 480/7 (1994).

For an unusual case under the 1975 Rules where the Arbitral Tribunal, with its seat of arbitration in Mexico City, named an expert on New York law but did not reveal his identity to the parties nor permit him to be questioned, *see* International Standard Electric Corporation (ISEC v. Bridas, 745 F. Supp. 172 (S.D.N.Y. 1990)) (objection to enforcement because of unfair procedure denying rights of defense, denied on the basis of failure of the party to object to the procedure during the arbitration).

J.F. Poudret, "Expertise et droit d'être entendu dans l'arbitrage international", *in* Études de Droit International en l'honneur de Pierre Lalive, Bâle (1993), pp. 608, 614-16.

20(5) At any time during the proceedings, the Arbitral Tribunal may summon any party to provide additional evidence.

PRIOR TEXT: NEW

MODIFICATION: N.A.

COMMENT: This addition follows the example of the AAA International Rules (Article 19), the LCIA Rules (Article 13), the ICSID Rules (Article 34), the UNCITRAL Rules (Article 24) and the CPR Rules (Article 2), which provide that the arbitral tribunal may, at any time during the arbitral proceedings, require the parties to produce additional evidence (*e.g.* documents, exhibits, etc.). While under the 1975 Rules the Arbitral Tribunal could order discovery from a party under the general power "to establish the facts of the case by all appropriate means", the new provision makes specific the arbitral power to order a party to produce evidence and dispels any doubt on the subject. It also reflects the increasing number of requests for document production in ICC arbitration.

OTHER REFERENCES:

C.P.& P., section 8.09.

See S. Jarvin, "Aspects of the Arbitral Proceedings", *ICC Bull.* Supp. 38, 40 (1997).

20(6) The Arbitral Tribunal may decide the case solely on the documents submitted by the parties unless any of the parties requests a hearing.

PRIOR TEXT: Article 14(3), 1975 Rules

Article 14(3)

The arbitrator may decide the case on the relevant documents alone if the parties so request or agree.

MODIFICATION: The provision "if the parties so request or agree" is replaced by "unless any of the parties requests a hearing". "[R]elevant documents" is replaced by the less subjective "documents submitted by the parties". "[S]olely" is used in place of "alone".

COMMENT: The arbitrator should have the power to decide the case based on the relevant documents alone, even if not requested to do so by the parties. If neither party requests a hearing, but have not expressly requested that the tribunal decide the case without a hearing, the tribunal retains the right to make such decision itself. In a default proceeding, for example, the parties might fail to "request or agree" that the case be concluded without a hearing, but the tribunal, according to practice, would have the right, after giving the parties a reasonable amount of time to request a hearing, to decide the case on the relevant documents alone. While the 1975 Rules permitted "documents only" arbitration and the 1998 Revision emphasizes the possibility, in fact "documents only" ICC arbitrations are rare; most of the contracts which contain ICC clauses are of a size or complexity sufficient to warrant that at least one of the parties will request a hearing.

OTHER REFERENCES:

C.P.&P., Sec. 23.01, "Arbitrator's power to establish facts by all appropriate means".

See ICC Arbitration No. 1512, I *Yearbook* 128 (1976), V *Yearbook* 170, 174 (1980) (denial of sole arbitrator of party's request to hear witnesses in view of copious documentary evidence, awards sustained Court of Appeal (England), [1978], 2 *Lloyd's L. Rep.* 223); cases described in C.P.&P., Sec. 23.01).

20(7) The Arbitral Tribunal may take measures for protecting trade secrets and confidential information.

PRIOR TEXT: NEW

MODIFICATION: N.A.

COMMENT: The issue of protecting trade secrets and confidential information revealed in the course of arbitral proceedings is only one aspect of the issue of general confidentiality of arbitral proceedings. The Court originally proposed that such a general obligation of confidentiality be included in the Rules and imposed on all persons associated with the arbitral process (*see* "OTHER REFERENCES" *infra*). The Working Party and the International Arbitration Commission, supported by comments of many of the National Committees, recognized that the requirements of national law concerning confidentiality of arbitral proceedings were in a state of development and conflict. *See, e.g.* Esso Australia Resources

Ltd. v. Plowman, High Court of Australia, 7 April 1955, No. 95 (814, XXI *Yearbook* 137 (1996)) where it was held that parties to an arbitration are not held to an implied obligation of confidentiality preventing them from transmitting documents received in an arbitration to third parties.   They considered it dangerous to have the ICC set out mandatory rules of conduct which it would have no power to enforce (consider, for instance, the status of a third party witness) and which might be in conflict with relevant national laws (as, for instance, when a party, pursuant to subpoena or otherwise, would be required to communicate arbitration documents to a third party).   A number of National Committees supported a general confidentiality amendment.   Others, while recognizing the private nature of ICC arbitral proceedings, took the view that as international arbitration has become the usual method of resolving international commercial disputes it is increasingly likely that participants in arbitration may have a legitimate interest, and in some instances may be required, to reveal the existence or results of an arbitration or information that became known as a result of arbitral proceedings.

The revision restricts itself to providing that the Arbitral Tribunal may take measures for protecting trade secrets and confidential information, accordingly dealing with concrete issues, principally that of how evidence presented in the arbitral proceedings relating to information which by its nature is confidential may be protected from disclosure.

The parties may by special agreement make specific provisions for confidentiality of the arbitration.   This may be agreed in the arbitration agreement or in the Terms of Reference.

OTHER REFERENCES:

Other provisions regarding confidentiality are found in Article 21(3) insuring the privacy of arbitral proceedings ("persons not involved in the proceedings shall not be admitted"), in Article 1 of the Internal Rules of the Court, "Confidential Character of the Work of the International Court of Arbitration", and in Article 3 of the 1998 Internal Rules (Court Members' obligation not to communicate to National Committees information concerning individual arbitrations which they have obtained through their status as Court Members).

The Court recommended that the following sub-section be added

> Unless otherwise agreed by the parties, they and their counsel, the arbitrators, experts and any other persons associated with the arbitration proceeding shall respect the confidentiality of all information and documents produced during such proceedings, provided that such information or documents are not in the public domain by virtue of a law or judicial decision or not otherwise necessary in order for a party or third party to establish its rights. This obligation of confidentiality extends in the same manner to awards .

Because of the nature of the disputes that it treats, the World Intellectual Property Organization provides the most elaborate provisions for confidentiality in the arbitrations it supervises.   *See* WIPO Rules, Articles 73 to 76 entitled:

"Confidentiality of the Existence of the Arbitration"; "Confidentiality of Disclosures Made During the Arbitration"; "Confidentiality of the Award"; "Maintenance of Confidentiality by the Center and Arbitrator".

See J. Paulsson and N. Rawding, "The Trouble with Confidentiality", 5 *ICC Bull.* No. 1, p. 48 (1994).

See E. Schwartz, "The Rights and Duties of ICC Arbitrators" in The Status of the Arbitrator, *ICC Bull.* (Special Supplement, 1995) 67, 92-5.

See M. Collins, Q.C., "Privacy and confidentiality in Arbitration Proceedings", 30 *Texas Int'l L.J.* 12 (1995).

See also, 11 *Arb. Int'l* No. 3 (1995), Special Issue on the Confidentiality of International Commercial Arbitration.

ICC arbitrators should be aware that they are considered to have an ethical obligation not to reveal information concerning an arbitration. *See e.g.* IBA Ethics, Art. 9:

> The deliberations of the arbitral tribunal, and the contents of the award itself, remain confidential in perpetuity unless the parties release the arbitrators from this obligation. An arbitrator should not participate in, or give any information for the purpose of assistance in, any proceedings to consider the award unless, exceptionally, he considers it his duty to disclose any material misconduct or fraud on the part of his fellow arbitrators.

Article 21
Hearings

21(1) When a hearing is to be held, the Arbitral Tribunal, giving reasonable notice, shall summon the parties to appear before it on the day and at the place fixed by it.

PRIOR TEXT: Article 15(1), 1975 Rules

Article 15(1)

At the request of one of the parties or if necessary on his own initiative, the arbitrator, giving reasonable notice, shall summon the parties to appear before him on the day and at the place appointed by him and shall so inform the Secretariat of the International Court of Arbitration.

MODIFICATION: "At the request of one of the parties or if necessary on its own initiative" is replaced with "When a hearing is to be held, the Arbitral Tribunal". The concluding provision of the 1975 Rules' Article 15(1) "and shall so inform the Secretariat of the International Court of Arbitration" is omitted.

COMMENT: Semantic changes have been made to shorten and simplify the subsection.

OTHER REFERENCES:

C.P.&P., Chapter 25, "Hearings".

21(2) If any of the parties, although duly summoned, fails to appear without valid excuse, the Arbitral Tribunal shall have the power to proceed with the hearing.

PRIOR TEXT: Article 15(2), 1975 Rules

Article 15(2)

If one of the parties, although duly summoned, fails to appear, the arbitrator, if he is satisfied that the summons was duly received and the party is absent without valid excuse, shall have power to proceed with the arbitration, and such proceedings shall be deemed to have been conducted in the presence of all parties.

MODIFICATION: The order of the sentence has been revised. The phrase "if he is satisfied that the summons was duly received and the party is absent. . . ", and the phrase ". . . and such proceedings shall be deemed to have been conducted in the presence of both parties" have been omitted.

COMMENT: No substantive changes are intended in this article which continues to empower the Tribunal to proceed by default. The "deeming" provision of the 1975 Rules was considered to be a confusing and redundant attempt to characterize the default proceeding in a way favorable to its recognition by certain courts. The revised article makes clear that the arbitrator, as agreed by the parties by their acceptance of the Rules, has the power to proceed when a party, although duly summoned, has not appeared, and such a hearing and any ensuing award will not be invalidated by the party's absence.

OTHER REFERENCES:

Article 3 of the Rules sets out what constitutes "duly summoning" a party.

See also Article 6(3) of the Rules, which provides generally for the arbitration to proceed in the default of one of the parties, and comment thereunder.

21(3) The Arbitral Tribunal shall be in full charge of the hearings, at which all the parties shall be entitled to be present. Save with the approval of the Arbitral Tribunal and the parties, persons not involved in the proceedings shall not be admitted.

PRIOR TEXT: Article 15(4), 1975 Rules

Article 15(4)

The arbitrator shall be in full charge of the hearings, at which all the parties shall be entitled to be present. Save with the approval of the arbitrator and of the parties, persons not involved in the proceedings shall not be admitted.

MODIFICATION: The sub-subsection is unmodified with the exception of reference to the "Arbitral Tribunal" in lieu of to the "arbitrator".

COMMENT: By adopting the ICC Rules to govern the resolution of their dispute, the parties agree that the proceedings shall be private. Unlike at judicial proceedings, members of the public have no right to attend.

OTHER REFERENCES:

See also Article 20(7) and the comments and references thereunder concerning confidentiality.

21(4) The parties may appear in person or through duly authorized representatives. In addition, they may be assisted by advisers.

PRIOR TEXT: Article 15(5), 1975 Rules

15(5) The parties may appear in person or through duly accredited agents. In addition, they may be assisted by advisers.

MODIFICATION: The term "duly accredited agents" is replaced by "duly authorized representatives".

COMMENT: The change has been effected in order to clarify the terminology used in the subsection. An arbitral tribunal may ask for proof that an alleged representative of a party has in fact been duly authorized to act for the party. Similar proof may be asked of an adviser who most frequently will be a lawyer for the party although legal qualification is not required and parties to ICC arbitration have full freedom to choose whosoever they wish as advisers. It is generally accepted, and appears to be true at present in almost all the major international arbitration centers, that a foreign lawyer may represent his client in international arbitration without infringing on any local mandatory law at the place of arbitration concerning the practice of law. The situation should be verified in each case, however. A description of the rights of representation and legal assistance for most jurisdictions is contained in ICCA International Council for Commercial Arbitration ("ICCA"), International Handbook on Commercial Arbitration (P. Sanders and A.J. Van den Berg, general editors), Kluwer, the Hague.

OTHER REFERENCES:

C.P.&P., Section 16.05, "Right of Audience".

Article 22
Closing of the Proceedings

22(1)When it is satisfied that the parties have had a reasonable opportunity to present their cases, the Arbitral Tribunal shall declare the proceedings closed. Thereafter, no further submission or argument may be made, or evidence produced, unless requested or authorized by the Arbitral Tribunal.

PRIOR TEXT: NEW

MODIFICATION: N.A.

COMMENT: Difficulties have developed in ICC practice over the years due to the late submission of evidence or argument following hearings, which could delay the deliberation of the arbitrators and the rendering of an award. An Arbitral Tribunal was sometimes faced with the dilemma of whether to refuse the material (leaving open the possibility of a challenge to the award on the ground that the party had not been able to present its case) or to accept it and the possible further delays occasioned by reply, rejoinder, etc. By setting out the "closing of the proceedings" as a mandatory decision to be made by the Arbitral Tribunal, the Rules attempt to impose some rigor in the post-hearing calendar for arbitral proceedings.

Note that this provision does not require the Arbitral Tribunal to give notice to the parties of its intention to close the proceedings at some future date. Where post-hearing briefs are not considered necessary or appropriate the Arbitral Tribunal could very well, at the close of the hearing, declare the proceedings closed.

After the closure of the proceedings, nothing prevents the arbitral tribunal from asking a party to furnish a further document or information. However, a party may not provide further documents, information or argument without having been previously authorized by the tribunal (*see* comments at meeting of Commission of International Arbitration of 21 March 1996, ICC Doc. 420/340 of 13 May 1996, p. 4).

For further information on "reasonable opportunity" *see* Article 15(2), *supra* and comments thereunder.

OTHER REFERENCES:

C.P.&P., Section 25.06, "Closing the hearings".

ICSID Arbitration Rules: Article 38

    Closure of the Proceedings

(1) When the presentation of a case by the parties is completed, the proceedings shall be declared closed.

(2) Exceptionally, the Tribunal may, before the award has been rendered, reopen the proceedings on the ground that new evidence is forthcoming of such a nature as to constitute a decisive factor, or that there is a vital need for clarification on certain specific points.

22(2) When the Arbitral Tribunal has declared the proceedings closed, it shall indicate to the Secretariat an approximate date by which the draft Award will be submitted to the Court for approval pursuant to Article 27. Any postponement of that date shall be communicated to the Secretariat by the Arbitral Tribunal.

PRIOR TEXT: NEW

MODIFICATION: N.A.

COMMENT: This subsection of Article 22 was incorporated into the Rules with the aim of expediting the arbitral process. The fixing of an approximate date by which the draft award should be submitted to the Court (which remains undisclosed to the parties) leads to increased calendar discipline by the arbitrators and should reduce post- hearing delay in the rendering of an award. The provision is of an administrative nature.

OTHER REFERENCES:

Article 23
Conservatory and Interim Measures

23(1) Unless the parties have otherwise agreed, as soon as the file has been transmitted to it, the Arbitral Tribunal may, at the request of a party, order any interim or conservatory measure it deems appropriate. The Arbitral Tribunal may make the granting of any such measure subject to appropriate security being furnished by the requesting party. Any such measure shall take the form of an order, giving reasons, or of an Award, as the Arbitral Tribunal considers appropriate.

PRIOR TEXT: NEW

MODIFICATION: N.A.

COMMENT: The addition of this subparagraph, and the revision of the Article as a whole, was effected to conform to current practice and the needs of modern international commercial arbitration. While ICC arbitrators have regularly granted conservatory and interim measures in the past, in appropriate circumstances, the 1975 Rules strangely enough did not affirmatively set out such a power. Rather, it was only by the negative implication of Article 8(5) of the 1975 Rules (full text set out under Article 23(2), below), which empowered the parties before the file was transmitted to the Arbitral Tribunal (and in exceptional circumstances even thereafter) to seek interim and conservatory measures from a Court, that it was implied that the parties could seek them from the Arbitral Tribunal as soon as it was constituted and the file was transmitted to it.

The present Rules make clear that in the event of a request for interim or conservatory measures from the Arbitral Tribunal, it has the power, under the Rules, to accord such requests.

Conservatory measures include those designed to preserve proof for use in the arbitration or preserve property or goods the subject of the agreement. Interim measures might more generally be designed to preserve the status quo pending arbitration or enjoin conduct likely to cause irreparable harm concerning the subject matter of the dispute (such as, for instance, the calling of bank guarantees provided for in a construction contract where the call would be contrary to the provisions of the contract).

Article 23(1) recognizes that the granting of a conservatory or interim measure might cause costs or losses to the party against whom it is ordered either because the petitioner's substantive claim fails on the merits or because the interim relief goes beyond what is finally awarded. Any such damage can be remedied in the final award by dispositions in favor of the party so injured. However, to be sure that the possible rights of the party against whom a conservatory or interim measure has been ordered are effectively protected, the Article provides that the

Tribunal may make its order "subject to appropriate security being furnished by the requesting party".

A separate issue, unrelated to the express power of the Tribunal to order security for interim or conservatory measures, is whether it may, as an interim measure, and as a condition for proceeding with the matter, order a party to provide security for the advances on arbitration costs, as well as the reasonable legal costs, which the other party will be expected to have suffered in the course of the proceedings. Article 31 provides that the Tribunal shall fix and apportion the costs of arbitration in its final award and that it has the discretionary power to order the losing party to pay all or part of the reasonable legal costs incurred by the winning party.

Article 23(1) does not specifically refer to the security for legal costs issue but it is quite clear that the broad power to "order any interim or conservatory measure", which was added to fill a recognized lacuna in the 1975 Rules, is sufficiently wide to give the Tribunal appropriate powers to order a party to put up security for the legal costs the other party may incur in defending what might be an unmeritorious claim. The drafters were quite aware of the repercussions of the *Ken-Ren* case in England where an English court intervened to grant security for costs, one of its grounds being that an ICC Arbitral Tribunal did not under the 1975 Rules have any power to do so. It is doubtful that ICC Arbitral Tribunals, even though having the power, will frequently be persuaded to grant security for legal costs as the device is not familiar to many legal systems.

Article 23(1) specifies that the Tribunal may make its decision in the form of an order or an award as appropriate. If the Arbitral Tribunal makes an award (which it may sometimes feel compelled to do in the interests of providing a title subject to execution by national courts) it must be submitted to the Court for scrutiny pursuant to the provisions set out in Article 27, and accordingly the advantage of an urgent or expeditive order may be lost. The more usual form will be that of an order. While Arbitral Tribunals do not have enforcement powers they may take into account the disregard by a party of such orders and voluntary compliance should occur quite regularly. The power of national courts to enforce interim measures ordered by arbitral tribunals varies from jurisdiction to jurisdiction.

OTHER REFERENCES:

The Court recommended that the following subsection be added:

> Upon receipt of the file and at the request of a party, the arbitrator may order any interim or conservatory measures.

C.P. & P., sec. 26.05, "Other interlocutory relief".

See M. Blessing, "Keynotes on Arbitral Decision Making", *ICC Bull.* Supp. (1997) ("The Working Party preferred not to make any specific reference in this respect, but the wording of Article 23 would seem broad enough to allow the making of an application for and the issuing of a ruling by the Tribunal on, the security for costs.").

See "Conservatory and Provisional Measures in International Arbitration", ICC Pub. No. 519 (1993) (Proceedings of joint ICC/AAA/ICSID colloquium on international arbitration held in Paris on 6 November 1992).

See R. Briner, "Interim Awards", 25 *International Business Lawyer* 153 (April, 1997) (examining the possibility of seeking an interim award on the issue of a party's obligation to advance its share of arbitration costs).

See D.A. Redfern, "Arbitration and the Courts: Interim Measures of Protection -Is the Tide about to Turn?", 30 Texas Int'l L.J. 71 (1995)

On the issue of an arbitral tribunal's power to grant security for costs and the relationship with national court residual powers *see* S.M. Coppee-Lavalin NV v. Ken-Ren Chemicals and Fertilizers Limited, [1995] 1 A.C.38, [1994] 2 All E.R. 449; D. Branson, "The Ken-Ren Case: It is an Ado Where More Aid Is Less Help", 10 *Arb. Int'l* 303 (1994); J. Paulsson, "The Unwelcome Atavism of Ken-Ren: The House of Lords Shows its Meddle", 1994 *Swiss Bull.* 439; Cl. Reymond, "Security for Costs in International Arbitration", 1994 *Law Quarterly Rev.* 501. Note that in England the court's power to order security for costs in arbitration was removed by the Arbitration Act of 1996.

See ICC Arbitration No. 6503 of 1990, 1995 *JDI* 1022, commentary Y.D. (Arbitral Tribunal ordered as a provisional measure that a long term contract should remain in existence, and the parties execute its terms, during a period of one year after a claimed date of rescission to permit the arbitral tribunal to rule on this issue on the merits and to avoid unnecessary damages. The commentary discusses the power of the arbitral tribunal to order interim measures and the reason for modifying the ICC rules to make this power explicit).

On the issue of the granting of security for costs by ICC arbitral tribunals, *see* ICC Arbitration No. 7489 of 1992, 1993 *JDI* 1078, note D.H. (Defendant counterclaimant requested tribunal to order Claimant to furnish a bank guarantee to pay defendant's legal costs and secure the value of its counterclaim as a condition to proceeding with the claim. Tribunal, with its seat in France, considered it had the power to order security, including security for costs, but found the request not justified); ICC Arbitration No. 7047 of 1994, 1995 *Swiss Bull.* 301 (refusal by tribunal to grant security for costs at the request of defendant state entities who had refused to contribute to ICC advance on costs of arbitration); ICC Arbitration No. 6697, 1992 *Rev. arb.* 142 (constitution of guarantee ordered by arbitral tribunal due to exceptional circumstances).

On the issue of enforcement of interim awards, *compare* Sperry International Trade v. Government of Israel 689 F.2d 301 (2d Cir 1982) (interim AAA award ordering a party to pay into an escrow account, pending final award, proceeds of a letter of credit intended to guarantee performance of a contract enforced by court) with Resort Condominiums International, Inc. v. Ray Bolwell and Resort Condominiums (Australasia) Pty. Ltd, Supreme Court of Queensland, 29 October 1993, MOT. No. 389 of 1993, 20 *Yearbook* 628 *(1995)* (interim AAA Arbitration Order and Award made in the United States granting certain injunctive relief pending final award was not a final foreign award subject to execution in Australia).

23(2) Before the file is transmitted to the Arbitral Tribunal, and in appropriate circumstances even thereafter, the parties may apply to any competent judicial authority for interim or conservatory measures. The application of a party to a judicial authority for such measures or for the implementation of any such measures ordered by an Arbitral Tribunal shall not be deemed to be an infringement or a waiver of the arbitration agreement and shall not affect the relevant powers reserved to the Arbitral Tribunal. Any such application and any measures taken by the judicial authority must be notified without delay to the Secretariat. The Secretariat shall inform the Arbitral Tribunal thereof.

PRIOR TEXT: Article 8(5), 1975 Rules

Article 8(5)

Before the file is transmitted to the arbitrator, and in exceptional circumstances even thereafter, the parties shall be at liberty to apply to any competent judicial authority for interim or conservatory measures, and they shall not by so doing be held to infringe the agreement to arbitrate or to affect the relevant powers reserved to the arbitrator.

Any such application and any measure taken by the judicial authority must be notified without delay to the Secretariat of the International Court of Arbitration,. The Secretariat shall inform the arbitrator thereof.

MODIFICATION: The term "arbitrator" is replaced by "Arbitral Tribunal". After the file is transmitted to the Arbitral Tribunal the parties may apply to a court in "appropriate" rather than "exceptional" circumstances as under the 1975 Rules. It is added to the amended article that a party may apply to a court for interim measures directly "or for the implementation of any such measures ordered by an Arbitral Tribunal". The subsection is reorganized but the content otherwise remains the same.

COMMENT: The above-referred changes are intended to clarify rather than change the sense of the Article. *See* comments on Article 23(1). The effect of the combination of Article 23(1) and 23(2) is that a party will normally address itself to the Arbitral Tribunal after it has been constituted. Many circumstances (including the fact that the Arbitral Tribunal does not have the power directly to enforce its mandate) may make it appropriate for a party to seek relief from a court either directly or to enforce an arbitrator's order.

OTHER REFERENCES:

C.P.&P, Chapter 27, "Ancillary Proceedings Before National Courts".

See "OTHER REFERENCES" at Article 23(1), *supra*.

AWARDS

Article 24
Time Limit for the Award

24(1) The time limit within which the Arbitral Tribunal must render its final Award is six months. Such time limit shall start to run from the date of the last signature by the Arbitral Tribunal or of the parties of the Terms of Reference, or, in the case of application of Article 18(3), the date of the notification to the Arbitral Tribunal by the Secretariat of the approval of the Terms of Reference by the Court.

PRIOR TEXT: Article 18(1), 1975 Rules

Article 18(1)

The time-limit within which the arbitrator must render his award is fixed at six months. Once the terms of Article 9(4) have been satisfied, such time-limit shall start to run from the date of the last signature by the arbitrator or of the parties of the document mentioned in Article 13 [the Terms of Reference], or from the expiry of the time-limit granted to a party by virtue of Article 13(2), or from the date that the Secretary General of the International Court of Arbitration notifies the arbitrator that the advance on costs is paid in full, if such notification occurs later.

MODIFICATIONS: The term "arbitrator" is replaced by "Arbitral Tribunal". The word "final" is added before "award" in the first sentence of the modified Rules. The term "final" in this context means the last award that the Tribunal is to render (and not an interim or partial award, even though these awards may be final in respect to the issues they resolve, *see* Article 27, 31 (3)). The time limit now starts to run independent of verification that the advance on costs has been satisfied (reference to Article 9(4) of the 1975 Rules and to notification by the Secretary General to the arbitrator of payment, is deleted). For text of prior Article 9(4) *see* Prior Text at Article 30(4), *supra*. The reference to the date of entry into effect of the Terms in the case of default, as running from the date of expiry of a time limit for the party to sign, is deleted as this supplemental procedure, and further delay associated therewith, has not been carried over from Article 18(1), 1975 Rules.

COMMENT: Reference to Article 9(4) of the 1975 Rules (verification whether the request for advance on costs had been complied with) is deleted as part of the general movement to disassociate the nonpayment of advances on costs from automatic blocking of the progress of the arbitration. Sufficient power to avoid the possibility that the Arbitral Tribunal will perform its mission without there being funds available to pay it is found in Article 30(4) (possible suspension of the proceeding by the Secretary General after consultation with the Arbitral Tribunal and dismissal of a claim or counterclaim) and Article 28(1) (non-notification of an award that has been made until costs are paid).

OTHER REFERENCES:

C.P. & P., Sec. 19.01, "Time limits for Awards".

See Bruna, "Control of Time Limits by the International Court of Arbitration", 7 *ICC Bull.* No. 2, 72 (1996).

24(2) The Court may extend this time limit pursuant to a reasoned request from the Arbitral Tribunal or on its own initiative if it decides it is necessary to do so.

PRIOR TEXT: Article 18(2), 1975 Rules

Article 18(2)

The Court may, pursuant to a reasoned request from the arbitrator or if need be on its own initiative, extend this time-limit if it decides it is necessary to do so.

MODIFICATIONS: The subsection is reorganized slightly.

COMMENT: As in the case of Article 18(2), (the entering into effect of the Terms of Reference) the Court's power to extend different time limits upon which the parties may agree (*e.g.* in expedited arbitration cases) must be considered. The specific power of the Court to extend the time for the rendering of a final award is an example of a power which is granted, more generally, by Article 32.

OTHER REFERENCES:

The Court recommended that the following sentence be added:

> In the same manner, the Court may decide to extend any other time limit fixed by the parties.

See S. Bruna, "Control of Time Limits by the International Court of Arbitration", 7 *ICC Bull.* No. 2, 72 (1996) (commenting on the practice of the Court in extending the six month period for the Arbitral Tribunal to render its award).

Article 25
Making of the Award

25(1) When the Arbitral Tribunal is composed of more than one arbitrator, an Award is given by a majority decision. If there be no majority, the Award shall be made by the chairman of the Arbitral Tribunal alone.

PRIOR TEXT: Article 19, 1975 Rules

Article 19

When three arbitrators have been appointed, the award is given by a majority decision. If there be no majority, the award shall be made by the Chairman of the arbitral tribunal alone.

MODIFICATION: "When more than one arbitrator has been appointed" is replaced by "When the Arbitral Tribunal is composed of more than one arbitrator".

COMMENT: The possibility for the Chairman to render an award alone where it is impossible to rally a majority is an effective device which prevents blockage of the arbitral process. In view of the possibility of extreme and divergent positions taken by party nominated arbitrators it is a useful procedural device, not provided for in many other institutional arbitration rules. It has not been necessary to use the procedure frequently, but its mere existence may have promoted agreement amongst the arbitrators or at least led one of the arbitrators to form a majority with the Chairman.

A similar provision is found in the LCIA Rules, but the UNCITRAL Rules, used by the Iran-U.S. Claims Tribunal, do not have such a device. As a result, many cases before the highly politicized Iran-U.S. Claims Tribunal remained without decision for very long periods of time due to the widely diverging views of the party appointed arbitrators and the reluctance of each of them to join the "middle-of-the-road" view of the Chairman.

The Rules permit, but do not encourage, the rendering of dissenting opinions. A dissenting opinion is not a part of the award but is communicated to the parties simultaneously with the award.

OTHER REFERENCES:

C.P. & P., "Majority awards and awards rendered by the chairman".

LCIA Rules, Article 16.3:

> Where there is more than one arbitrator and they fail to agree on any issue, they shall decide by a majority. Failing a majority decision on any issue, the Chairman of the Tribunal shall make the award alone as if he were sole arbitrator . . . .

UNCITRAL Rules of Arbitration, Article 31:

> (1) When there are three arbitrators, any award or other decision of the arbitral tribunal shall be made by a majority of the arbitrators.

> (2) In the case of questions of procedure, when there is no majority or when the arbitral tribunal so authorizes, the presiding arbitrator may decide on his own, subject to revision, if any, by the arbitral tribunal.

See F.P. Donovan, *"Dissenting Opinions"*, *7 ICC Bull.* No. 2, 76 (1996).

See Working Party of the ICC Commission on International Arbitration (M. Hunter, Chairman), "Final Report on Dissenting and Separate Opinions", 2 *ICC Bull.* No. 1, 32 (1991), reprinted in II C.P.&P, Appendix V (Looseleaf edition).

25(2) The Award shall state the reasons upon which it is based.

PRIOR TEXT: NEW

MODIFICATION: N.A.

COMMENT: The 1975 Rules did not, by their terms, require an Arbitral Tribunal to give reasons for its award; nevertheless arbitral tribunals invariably did so. The reasoned award can be said to be a known characteristic of ICC arbitration. Without a reasoned award it would seem impossible for the Court to fulfill its mission of scrutiny of the award under Article 27. The revised Rules make explicit a requirement that was otherwise implicit.

OTHER REFERENCES:

C.P. & P., Sec. 19.04, "Form of Award".

LCIA Rules, Article 16.1:

> The Tribunal shall make its award in writing and, unless all the parties agree otherwise, shall state the reasons upon which its award is based. . . .

UNCITRAL Rules of Arbitration, Article 32(3):

> The arbitral tribunal shall state the reasons upon which the award is based, unless the parties have agreed that no reasons are to be given.

See M. Fontaine, "Drafting the Award: A Perspective from a Civil Law Jurist", 5 *ICC Bull.* No. 1, 30 (1994).

See H. Lloyd, "Writing Awards: A Common Lawyer's Perspective", 5 *ICC Bull.* No. 1, 38 (1994).

25(3) The Award shall be deemed to be made at the place of the arbitration and on the date stated therein.

PRIOR TEXT: Article 22, 1975 Rules

Article 22
Making of Award

The arbitral award shall be deemed to be made at the place of the arbitration proceedings and on the date when it is signed by the arbitrator.

MODIFICATION: "[A]rbitration proceedings" is replaced by "arbitration". The date upon which the arbitral award shall be deemed to be made is now set out as "the date stated therein", replacing "the date when it is signed by the arbitrator".

COMMENT: The modification was made in accordance with practice. Prior to signature by the arbitrators, a draft award is submitted to the Court for its scrutiny (*see* Article 27). After the Court's approval, the award is remitted to the arbitrators for signature (and corrections, where required). Since these signatures are frequently solicited by circulation of the award to the arbitrators, serially, it could be difficult to ascertain the date of the signature of the last arbitrator. The present revision provides that the date of the award, whether of a sole arbitrator or of a three man tribunal, will be stated in the award and will be considered to be the date thereof.

OTHER REFERENCES:

C.P. & P., Sec. 22.01, "Signature of the award by arbitrators".

Despite the provision in the 1975 Rules that an award should be deemed to be made at the place of arbitration, the English House of Lords found in Hiscox v. Outhwaite, [1991] 3 All E.R. 641 that an award in an ICC arbitration held at the place of arbitration in London should be considered a French award because it was signed in Paris by the President of the arbitral tribunal and was considered to be made there. This result has been changed by the English Arbitration Act 1996.

For a decision relying on the text of former Article 22 (as well as the text of former Article 24) finding that the time within which an application to confirm an award must be brought under the Federal Arbitration Act runs from the date of the "making" of the award (and not from the date at which any right of judicial recourse at the place of arbitration expires) *see* Seetransport Wiking Trader v. Navimpex Centrala, 989 F. 2d 572 (2nd Cir. 1993).

Article 6, 1998 Internal Rules [Appendix II]

Note that the Internal Rule concerning the scrutiny of arbitral awards has been modified from the 1980 version. In connection with its scrutiny of the award the Court is to consider the requirements of the "mandatory law" [not "mandatory rules"] at the "place of arbitration" but now only "to the extent practicable".

The Court acts under the general mandate, as provided in Article 35 of the Rules to "make every effort to make sure that the award is enforceable at law". At the same time, as this revision of the Internal Rules shows, it does not wish to be hemmed in by formalistic procedural requirements and wishes to retain the maximum discretion in how to best assure the enforceability of the award (it being recognized that the place of enforcement will frequently be some other place other than the place of arbitration).

Article 26
Award by Consent

If the parties reach a settlement after the file has been transmitted to the Arbitral Tribunal in accordance with Article 13, the settlement shall be recorded in the form of an Award made by consent of the parties if so requested by the parties and the Arbitral Tribunal agrees to do so.

PRIOR TEXT: Article 17, 1975 Rules

Article 17

If the parties reach a settlement after the file has been transmitted to the arbitrator in accordance with Article 10, the same shall be recorded in the form of an arbitral award made by consent of the parties.

MODIFICATION: "Arbitrator" is replaced by "Arbitral Tribunal". The Article reference number is modified. "Award" replaces "arbitral award". The revision provides that the settlement "if so requested by the parties and if the Arbitral Tribunal agrees to do so" may be recorded in the form of an award.

COMMENT: The revision makes clear that the arbitrators have discretion not to record a settlement as an award if they deem it would be inappropriate to do so. This would be the case in the rare event that they considered that the parties were seeking to achieve an illegitimate purpose with the award such as using it as an instrument of fraud.

OTHER REFERENCES:

C.P. & P., Sec. 19.02, "Awards by consent".

Article 27
Scrutiny of the Award by the Court

Before signing any Award, the Arbitral Tribunal shall submit it in draft form to the Court. The Court may lay down modifications as to the form of the Award and, without affecting the Arbitral Tribunal's liberty of decision, may also draw its attention to points of substance. No Award shall be rendered by the Arbitral Tribunal until it has been approved by the Court as to its form.

PRIOR TEXT: Article 21, 1975 Rules

Article 21

Before signing an award, whether partial or definitive, the arbitrator shall submit it in draft form to the International Court of Arbitration. The Court may lay down modifications as to the form of the award and, without affecting the arbitrator's liberty of decision, may also draw his attention to points of substance. No award shall be signed until it has been approved by the Court as to its form.

MODIFICATION: The qualifying phrase "whether partial or definitive" is omitted. All terms previously defined in Article 2 of the Rules now take their abbreviated form. "Arbitral Tribunal" is used in lieu of "arbitrator". "[B]y the Arbitral Tribunal" is appended to "No Award shall be rendered".

COMMENT: Article 2(iii) of the revised Rules provides: "'Award' includes, *inter alia*, an interim, partial or final award". All such awards must be submitted to the Court for scrutiny. The term "definitive award" is not found anywhere in the Rules and has been deleted. It presumably denoted the last award of the Tribunal disposing of all matters before it (*see* Article 31(3) where the term "final award" is used in the same sense).

Under Article 4(5) of the 1998 Internal Rules the three man Committee of the Court may take any decisions which the Court delegates to it. Under the prior Internal Rules, only the Court in Plenary Session had the power to scrutinize awards under Article 27. Pursuant to its power under Article 4(5) (a) of the new Internal Rules to determine those decisions that the Committee of the Court may take, the Court has empowered the Committee to scrutinize and approve certain awards, which will allow earlier notification to the parties. Awards which raise particular problems or difficulties will continue to be scrutinized and approved at a Plenary Session of the Court. *See* R. Briner, "The Implementation of the 1998 ICC Rules of Arbitration", 8 *ICC Bull.* No. 2, 7, 9 (1997).

OTHER REFERENCES:

C.P. & P., Chapter 20, "The Court's Scrutiny of Awards"; C.P. & P., Sec. 22.01, "Signature of the award by arbitrators".

See D. McGovern, "Scrutiny of the Award by the ICC Court", 5 *ICC Bull*. No. 1, 46 (1994).

See D. Hascher, "Scrutiny of Draft Awards by the Court: 1994 Overview", 6 *ICC Bull*. No. 1, 51 (1995).

See D. Hascher, "Scrutiny of Draft Awards by the Court: 1995 Overview", 7 *ICC Bull*. No. 1, 14 (1996).

See Compagnie des Bauxites de Guinée v. Hammermills (D.D.C. 1992), 1992 WestLaw 122712. After the draft award had been approved by the ICC, the arbitrator added $ 1 million in attorney's fees to be paid by the losing claimant. The federal district court confirmed the award, reasoning that no specific ICC Rules governed the procedures by which attorney's fees are awarded. The decision has been questioned, since omission of $1 million (not a *de minimis* amount) arguably impaired the substantial completeness expected of a draft award submitted to the ICC for scrutiny. The arbitrator's authority to fix attorney's fees is not unfettered since it is limited to "normal legal costs incurred by the parties". Such a determination should be subject to the Court's scrutiny.

Article 28
Notification, Deposit, and
Enforceability of the Award

28(1) Once an Award has been made, the Secretariat shall notify to the parties the text signed by the Arbitral Tribunal, provided always that the costs of the arbitration have been fully paid to the ICC by the parties or by one of them.

PRIOR TEXT: Article 23(1), 1975 Rules

Article 23(1)

Once an award has been made, the Secretariat shall notify to the parties the text signed by the arbitrator; provided always that the costs of the arbitration have been fully paid to the International Chamber of Commerce by the parties or by one of them.

MODIFICATION: "Arbitral Tribunal" replaced "arbitrator". Previously defined terms are abbreviated.

COMMENT: This subsection provides a method for the Secretariat to ensure payment of the fees of the Arbitral Tribunal and the ICC's administrative fees. Retention of the Award serves as security for the payment of these costs. The device is complementary to the power of the Secretary General to order the suspension of arbitral proceedings when advances on costs have not been paid (*see* Article 30(4)).

OTHER REFERENCES:

C.P.&P., Section 22.02, "Payment of costs and notification of award to parties".

28(2) Additional copies certified true by the Secretary General shall be made available on request and at any time to the parties, but to no one else.

PRIOR TEXT: Article 23(2), 1975 Rules

Additional copies certified true by the Secretary General of the International Court of Arbitration shall be made available, on request and at any time, to the parties but to no one else.

MODIFICATION: Previously defined terms are abbreviated.

COMMENT: This subsection emphasizes the confidentiality inherent to ICC arbitration proceedings, in that the additional copies of the award are available on request to parties, but "to no one else".

OTHER REFERENCES:

See Internal Rules, Article 5, concerning the power of the Secretary General to delegate certification powers to the General Counsel and Deputy Secretary General of the Court.

28(3) By virtue of the notification made in accordance with Paragraph 1 of this Article, the parties waive any other form of notification or deposit on the part of the Arbitral Tribunal.

PRIOR TEXT: Article 23(3), 1975 Rules

(3) By virtue of the notification made in accordance with paragraph 1 of this article, the parties waive any other form of notification or deposit on the part of the arbitrator.

MODIFICATION: "Arbitral Tribunal" replaces "arbitrator".

COMMENT: N.A.

OTHER REFERENCES:

28(4) An original of each Award made in accordance with the present Rules shall be deposited with the Secretariat.

PRIOR TEXT: First sentence of Article 25, 1975 Rules

Article 25

An original of each award made in accordance with the present Rules shall be deposited with the Secretariat of the International Court of Arbitration.

MODIFICATION: Previously defined terms take their abbreviated forms.

COMMENT: An original of the award is deposited with the Secretariat in its nature of a permanent institution.

OTHER REFERENCES:

C.P.&P., Section 22.04, "Deposit of award and assistance of secretariat".

28(5) The Arbitral Tribunal and the Secretariat shall assist the parties in complying with whatever further formalities may be necessary.

PRIOR TEXT: Second sentence of Article 25, 1975 Rules

The arbitrator and the Secretariat of the Court shall assist the parties in complying with whatever further formalities may be necessary

MODIFICATION: "Arbitral Tribunal" replaces "arbitrator". Previously defined terms take their abbreviated forms.

COMMENT: N.A.

OTHER REFERENCES:

C.P.&P., "Section 22.04, "Deposit of award and assistance of secretariat".

28(6) Every Award shall be binding on the parties. By submitting the dispute to arbitration under these Rules, the parties undertake to carry out any Award without delay and shall be deemed to have waived their right to any form of recourse insofar as such waiver can validly be made.

PRIOR TEXT: Article 24(1), 24(2) 1975 Rules

(1) The arbitral award shall be final.

(2) By submitting the dispute to arbitration by the International Chamber of Commerce, the parties shall be deemed to have undertaken to carry out the resulting award without delay and to have waived their right to any form of appeal insofar as such waiver can validly be made.

MODIFICATION: The first sentence of Article 24, 1975 Rules has been revised to provide that "Every Award shall be binding on the parties" instead of "shall be final". The parties are deemed to have waived "their right to any form of recourse" instead of "their right to any form of appeal", as formerly provided in Article 24(2) of the 1975 Rules.

COMMENT: The modifications are not intended to change the substantive effect of Article 24 of the 1975 Rules. As set out in the title to Article 28 "Notification, Deposit, and Enforceability of the Award", it is the objective of the Rules to ensure enforceable awards (see *also* Article 35, "General Rule"). Any award (which includes, as defined in Article 2, *inter alia*, interim, partial and final awards) shall be considered to be binding on the parties, thus fulfilling the criteria for immediate enforceability under Articles III and V of the New York Convention.

The waiver of "any form of recourse" rather than "any form of appeal" was considered to be broader than the former language and more in accordance with the terminology of modern arbitration statutes which generally permit access to the courts for the review of arbitration awards only on exceptional grounds and do not permit "appeals" in which issues of law and fact may be relitigated. The modification is also consistent with the French language Rules which provide both in the 1975 and 1998 versions for the renunciation of "toutes voies de recours". "Recourse" would include "appeals" wherever they are permitted by national law. The extent to which recourse may be waived is a subject to be determined under the applicable national law.

The effect of the waiver of appeal will operate differently depending on the country in which arbitration is conducted. For example in England, Article 28 of the ICC Rules will exclude appeals on points of law. *See* Section 69 of the 1996 Arbitration Act. A similar result was obtained under prior law.   *See* Arab

African Energy Corp. (Arafenco). v. Olieprodukten Nederland B.V., Q.B. [1983] 2 *Lloyd's Rep* 419. However, challenge for excess of authority or serious procedural irregularity may not be excluded by contract. *See* Sections 67 and 68 of the 1996 Act. In Switzerland, under federal arbitration law waiver of the right to challenge an award requires an explicit statement (*"déclaration expresse"*), which cannot be incorporated by reference to institutional rules. *See* Article 192, *LDIP*. If the parties elect cantonal law in Switzerland, any purported waiver of the appeal provided in Article 36 of the Intercantonal Concordat will be ineffective. In the United States, the ICC waiver rule has become relevant in litigation where language in an arbitration clause purported to *expand* rather than restrict the scope of judicial review.

OTHER REFERENCES:

C.P. & P., Sec. 22.03, "Finality and enforceability of award".

See W.L. Craig, "Uses and Abuses of Appeal", 4 *Arb. Int'l* 174 (1988).

See Lapine v. Kyocera, 130 F.3d 884, (9th cir. 1997), where the Court of Appeal reversed a District Court decision which had refused to give effect to the specific terms of an ICC arbitration clause calling for judicial review of conclusions of law that were "erroneous" and facts that were not supported by the evidence". The 2-1 appellate decision permitting the parties by agreement to expand the grounds of judicial review beyond those provided in the Federal Arbitration Act was controversial. However, its finding that the parties' specific agreement took precedence over the waiver of appeal provision in the prior version of the Rules was clearly right.

See Other References at Article 25(3).

Article 29
Correction and
Interpretation of the Award

29(1) On its own initiative, the Arbitral Tribunal may correct a clerical, computational or typographical error, or any errors of similar nature contained in an Award, provided such correction is submitted for approval to the Court within 30 days of the date of such Award.

PRIOR TEXT: NEW

MODIFICATION: N.A.

COMMENT: This provision was added in order to give the Arbitral Tribunal the power on its own initiative to correct errors of a non-substantive nature provided such corrections are made within thirty days of the award. The Arbitral Tribunal has the same power to act when requested to do so by a party (*see* Article 29(2)). The provisions are similar to those found in other international arbitration rules currently in use. In past practice there has been doubt whether an ICC Arbitral Tribunal had the power to correct an award, since after the draft award has been scrutinized and approved by the Court, signed by the Arbitral Tribunal and notified to the parties, it could be maintained that the Tribunal had fulfilled its mission and therefore was discharged. The Court nevertheless had in several cases permitted a Tribunal to correct an award. The present article now confirms this practice and sets out the thirty day time period following the award in which such a correction may be made, and the procedure for making it.

OTHER REFERENCES:

LCIA Rules, Article 17.1 and 17.2:

> 17.1 Within thirty days of receipt of the award. . . a party may by notice to the Registrar request the Tribunal to correct in the award an errors in computation, any clerical or typographical errors or any errors of similar nature. If the Tribunal considers the request to be justified, it shall make the corrections within thirty days of receipt of the request. Any correction, which shall take the form of a separate memorandum, shall become part of the award.

> 17.2 The Tribunal may correct any error of the type referred to in Article 17(1) on its own initiative within thirty days of the date of the award.

WIPO Rules, Article 66(a) and (b):

> (a) Within thirty days after receipt of the award, a party may, by notice to the Tribunal, with a copy to the Center and the other party, request the Tribunal to correct in the award any clerical, typographical or computational errors. If the Tribunal considers the request to be justified, it shall make the correction within 30 days after receipt of the request. Any correction, which shall take

the form of a separate memorandum, signed by the Tribunal in accordance with Article 62(d) shall become part of the award.

(b) The Tribunal may correct any error of the type referred to in paragraph (a) on its own initiative within 30 days after the date of the award.

UNCITRAL Rules, Article 36(1), 36(2):

(1) Within 30 days after receipt of the award either party, with notice to the other party, may request the arbitral tribunal to correct in the award any errors in computation, any clerical or typographical errors, or any errors of similar nature. The arbitral tribunal may within 30 days after the communication of the award make such corrections on its own initiative.

(2) Such corrections shall be in writing and the provisions of Article 32, paragraphs 2 to 7, shall apply.

See Kuhn, "Rectification and Interpretation of Arbitral Awards", 7 *ICC Bull.* No. 2, 78 (1996).

29(2) Any application of a party for the correction of an error of the kind referred to in Article 29(1), or for the interpretation of an Award, must be made to the Secretariat within 30 days of the receipt of the Award by such party, in a number of copies as stated in Article 3(1). After transmittal of the application to the Arbitral Tribunal, it shall grant the other party a short time limit, normally not exceeding 30 days, from the receipt of the application by that party to submit any comments thereon. If the Arbitral Tribunal decides to correct or interpret the Award, it shall submit its decision in draft form to the Court not later than 30 days following the expiration of the time limit for the receipt of any comments from the other party or within such other period as the Court may decide.

PRIOR TEXT: NEW

MODIFICATION: N.A.

COMMENT: Article 29(2) provides that the Arbitral Tribunal has, upon the application of any party within thirty days of the notification of the award, the same power to correct an award as it may exercise on its own initiative under Article 29(1).

Article 29(2) also permits an Arbitral Tribunal, upon the application of any party within thirty days of the notification of the award, to interpret the award and to issue a decision of interpretation in the form and under the conditions set out in Article 29(2).

The modification of the Rules to permit an Arbitral Tribunal to correct an award upon the request of a party or upon its own motion was not controversial. It confirmed a very limited practice which under the 1975 Rules had permitted correction of awards in exceptional circumstances. The power exists under most modern international arbitration rules.

The new power permitting the Arbitral Tribunal to interpret an award was, on the other hand, controversial. Those in opposition to the modification expressed fear that the power given to a party to request interpretation of an award could be used as a weapon for confusion and delay in the hands of a party disappointed by the outcome of the arbitral proceedings as reflected in the arbitral award. Modern arbitration rules are mixed in permitting this power of interpretation (the UNCITRAL, AAA International Rules, ICSID Rules, and Stockholm Rules do provide for interpretation; the LCIA, AAA Commercial, and WIPO Rules do not).

While the new Rules permit an Arbitral Tribunal to interpret an award upon the request of a party, protection from abuse is found in the following provisions: i) a party's application for an interpretation can only be made within thirty days of notification of the award; ii) only a very brief time period is provided for the parties to make their views known on the interpretation issue (the requesting party must give its views with its application within thirty days of the issuance of the award, the other party must comment within thirty days of receiving the application); iii) the tribunal is under no obligation to accept to render a decision interpreting the award; it has discretion whether or not to do so and may find it unnecessary or inappropriate to make an interpretation; iv) any decision interpreting an award becomes a part of the award and is subject to the scrutiny of the Court (*see* Article 29(3)).

The same protection exists for application for the correction of an award, where possibilities for abuse, however, are thought to be fewer.

It is an open question whether the Court of Arbitration, applying its broad discretionary powers under Article 35 (the "General Rule") could permit interpretation or correction of an award after the specific 30 day time limit provided in Article 29.

OTHER REFERENCES:

The Court recommended that the following subsection be added:

> Any application for the correction of a clerical, computational or typographical error in an award, or for its interpretation, must be communicated to the Secretariat within thirty days of the notification of such award to the parties. The Secretariat shall send a copy of such application to the other party and, within thirty days, to the arbitrator. The decision of the arbitrator is to be submitted to the Court in draft form, within the time-limit of thirty days, for scrutiny in accordance with Article 21.

AAA International Rules, Article 30(1):

> Within thirty days after the receipt of an award, any party, with notice to the other parties, may request the tribunal to interpret the award or correct any

clerical, typographical or computation errors or make an additional award as to claims presented but omitted from the award.

UNCITRAL Rules, Article 35

(1) "within 30 days after the receipt of the award, either party, with notice to the other party, may request that the arbitral tribunal give an interpretation of the award.

(2) the interpretation shall be given in writing within 45 days after the receipt of the request. The interpretation shall form part of the award and the provisions of article 32, paragraphs 2 to 7, shall apply".

See W. Kuhn, "Rectification and Interpretation of Arbitral Awards", 7 *ICC Bull.* No. 2, 78 (1996).

See R. Knutson, "The Interpretation of Arbitral Awards: When is a Final Award not Final", 11 *J. Int'l Arb.* No. 2, p. 99 (1994).

See P.Y. Gunter, "L'Interprétation de la Sentence: examen de quesques questions à la lumière d'un cas rèel", 1996 *Swiss. Bull.* 574.

See N. Garnier, "Interpréter, rectifier et compléter les sentences arbitrales internationales", 1995 *Rev. arb.* 565.

Although the 1975 Rules were indeed silent as to the power of the Arbitral Tribunal to correct or interpret awards, such silence should not have been seen as a total refusal on the part of the Arbitral Tribunal to correct or interpret an award. The addition of this article confirms a power that was previously available, though tacitly so. *See* Case N° 6653 (1993 obs. J.J. Arnaldez, 3 ICC Collection, 512).

See M. Buhler, "Correction and interpretation of Awards and Advances on Costs", *ICC Bull.* Supp. 53,54 (1997).

29(3) The decision to correct or to interpret the Award shall take the form of an addendum and shall constitute part of the Award. The provisions of Articles 25, 27 and 28 shall apply *mutatis mutandis*.

PRIOR TEXT: NEW

MODIFICATION: N.A.

COMMENT: *See* comments at Article 29(2). It is important to note that any correction or interpretation by the Arbitral Tribunal is subject to the same procedure as for the making of an Award (Article 25), Scrutiny of the Award by the Court (Article 27) and Notification, Deposit and Enforceability of the Award (Article 28).

OTHER REFERENCES:

COSTS

Article 30
Advance to Cover the Costs of the Arbitration

30(1) After receipt of the Request, the Secretary General may request the Claimant to pay a provisional advance in an amount intended to cover the costs of arbitration until the Terms of Reference have been drawn up.

PRIOR TEXT: NEW

MODIFICATION: N.A.

COMMENT: One of the criticisms of ICC arbitration has been the excessive lapse of time between the filing of the Request and the transmission of the file to the Arbitral Tribunal. This was due in the past to the necessity that the Court fix an advance on costs intended to cover the entire arbitral proceeding, a task which required study of the terms of the Request, the Answer, and any counterclaim or counterclaims contained therein, as well as the recommendation of the Secretary General concerning the advance to be established. The amount would then be set by a three man Committee of the Court. Pursuant to Article 9(3) of the 1975 Rules: "The Secretariat may make the transmission of the file to the arbitrator conditional upon the payment by the parties or one of them of the whole or part of the advance on costs to the International Chamber of Commerce".

Under regulations established by the Court and published with the 1975 Rules (Appendix III, Schedule of Conciliation and Arbitration Costs, in effect as of 1 January 1993, Article 2(b)) it was provided that, "The submission of any claim or counterclaim to the arbitrator(s) shall be made only after at least half of the advance on costs has been satisfied". By administrative practice the Secretariat would then call for the payment of one-half of the total advance on costs (estimated to be sufficient to cover arbitration costs down to the signature of the Terms of Reference) which the parties were asked to contribute in equal shares (*i.e.* each party would contribute 25% of the total advance set).

Accordingly, further delay could be expected after the fixing of the advance on costs by the Court, while awaiting payment by the defendant of its initial installment on the advance on costs. The modification in the new Rules provides for the circumventing of this elaborate procedure by permitting the Secretary General to set a provisional advance to be paid by the Claimant alone in an amount determined to be sufficient to cover arbitration costs down to the establishment of the Terms of Reference.

The power given to the Secretary General is not a requirement. Should the circumstances of the particular file indicate that no time would be gained by this procedure (or for any other reason that it might not be appropriate) the Secretary General may simply await the determination of the advance on costs by the Court pursuant to Article 30(2).

Note that any advance on costs set by the Secretary General under Article 30(1) is provisional only. The setting of the advance on costs to cover the arbitral proceedings is the domain of the Court (Article 30(2)). Any payment requested by the Secretary General shall be considered a partial payment of the advance on costs established by the Court (Article 30(3)).

As set out in Article 1(2) of the Schedule of Arbitration Costs and Fees (Appendix III), the provisional advance fixed by the Secretary General under the new Rules shall normally not exceed the amount obtained by adding together (i) the administrative expenses calculated by applying to the amount of the claim the scale for administrative fees set forth in Article 4(2)(a) of the 1998 Appendix III to the new Rules; (ii) the arbitral fees calculated by applying the minimum under the scale of arbitrator's fees set forth in Article 4(2)(b) of the 1998 Appendix III to the new Rules; and (iii) the expected reimbursable expenses incurred by the arbitral tribunal in the drafting of the terms of references .

The advance set by the Secretary General is based on the amount of Claimant's claim alone and does not cover any amount for any counter claim which may be filed by Respondent. Both the amount of the claims and the amount of the counter claims will be taken into account when the advance on costs is established by the Court under Article 30(2).

OTHER REFERENCES:

C.P.&P., Chapter 21, "Determination of Costs".

C.P.&P., Table 9B, "Estimating Costs and the Advance on Costs".

See M. Buhler, "Correction and Interpretation of Awards and Advances on Costs", *ICC Bull.* Supp. 53, 56–57 (1997).

30(2) As soon as practicable, the Court shall fix the advance on costs in an amount likely to cover the fees and expenses of the arbitrators and the ICC administrative costs for the claims and counterclaims which have been referred to it by the parties. This amount may be subject to readjustment at any time during the arbitration. Where, apart from the claims, counterclaims are submitted, the Court may fix separate advances on costs for the claims and the counterclaims.

PRIOR TEXT: Article 9(1), 1975 Rules

Article 9(1)

The International Court of Arbitration shall fix the amount of the advance on costs in a sum likely to cover the costs of arbitration of the claims which have been referred to it.

Where, apart from the principal claim, one or more counter-claims are submitted, the Court may fix separate advances on costs for the principal claim and the counter-claim or counter-claims.

MODIFICATION: In the first sentence, the phrase "as soon as practicable" has been added to the modified Rules. "[F]ees and expenses of the arbitrators and ICC administrative costs for the claims and counterclaims" replaces "costs of arbitration of the claims". The second sentence has been added. The term "principal claim" is now simply "claims".

COMMENT: The advance on costs is only intended to cover the ICC administrative costs and the fees and expenses of the arbitrators and not the fees and expenses of any expert which the Tribunal might appoint or legal costs and expenses which might be incurred by a party and claimed against the other party. This has been the consistent practice of the Court. The first sentence of Article 30(2) makes this clear. The prior text of Article 9(1) of the 1975 Rules, stating that the advance was intended to cover "the costs of arbitration", was misleading since these costs, finally determined by the Court at the end of the arbitration, are defined to include as well "the fees and expenses of any experts, appointed by the Arbitral Tribunal, and the reasonable legal and other costs incurred by the parties" (Article 20(2), 1975 Rules, Article 31, 1998 Rules).

The amount of the advance on costs may be readjusted at any time during the course of the proceedings either upward, or less frequently, downward. The Arbitral Tribunal should inform the Secretariat of new circumstances arising at any time throughout the proceedings which would be relevant to the Court's determination of whether the advance should be readjusted.

The express provision that the amount in dispute upon which the advance on costs is fixed takes into account both the amount of the claims and the amount of the counter claims is consistent with prior practice but clarifies it.

The effect of the Court's power in appropriate cases to fix separate advances for the claims and for the counterclaims is that where a party does not pay the fixed separate advance, the relevant claim or counterclaim will be considered as withdrawn (*see* Article 30(4)).

OTHER REFERENCES:

C.P. & P., Chapter 3, "Costs", Chapter 14, "Advance to Cover Costs".

See E. Schwartz, "The ICC Arbitral Process, Part IV: The Costs of ICC Arbitration", 4 *ICC Bull*. No. 1, 8 (1993).

See Extracts from ICC Awards on Arbitration Costs, 4 *ICC Bull*. No. 1, p. 31 (1993).

See D. Mitrovic, "Advance to Cover Costs of Arbitration", 7 *ICC Bull*. No. 2, 88 (1996).

See D. Byrne, "Payment of Advances on Fees to Arbitrators in ICC Proceedings", 7 *ICC Bull*. No. 2, 84 (1996).

30(3) The advance on costs fixed by the Court shall be payable in equal shares by the Claimant and the Respondent. Any provisional advance paid on the basis of Article 30(1) will be considered as a partial payment thereof. However, any party shall be free to pay the whole of the advance on costs in respect of the principal claim or the counterclaim should the other party fail to pay its share. When the Court has set separate advances on costs in accordance with Article 30(2), each of the parties shall pay the advance on costs corresponding to its claims.

PRIOR TEXT: Article 9(2), 1975 Rules; Article 14, 1980 Internal Rules

Article 9(2), 1975 Rules

The advance on costs shall be payable in equal shares by the Claimant or Claimants and the Defendant or Defendants. However, any one party shall be free to pay the whole of the advance on costs in respect of the claim or the counter-claim should the other party fail to pay its share.

Article 14, Internal Rules

When the International Court of Arbitration has set separate advances on costs for a specific case in accordance with Article 9(1) (sub para. 2) of the ICC Rules of Arbitration, the Secretariat requests each of the parties to pay the amount corresponding to its claims, without prejudice to the right of the parties to pay the said advances on costs in equal shares, if they deem it advisable.

MODIFICATIONS: The subsection now combines the provisions of Article 9(2) and the provision of Article 14 of the 1980 Internal Rules, which is now incorporated in the arbitration rules. The initial advance to be paid by the Claimant in an amount estimated by the Secretariat to cover arbitration costs through the Terms of Reference (a new provision of Article 30(1)) is considered a partial payment of the Claimant's share of the advance on costs fixed by the Court under Article 30(2). The provision of Article 9(2) of the 1975 Rules that any party may pay the entire amount of the advance on costs (and not only its "equal share") is carried forward, this being the usual method to thwart the dilatory tactics of a defendant. The provision of Article 14 of the 1980 Internal Rules providing that where separate advances on costs have been set for the principal claim and the counterclaim, the parties nonetheless have the right to "pay the said advances on costs in equal shares if they deem it advisable", has been eliminated.

COMMENT: The fact that any initial advance fixed by the Secretariat under Article 30(1) and paid by the Claimant shall be considered a partial payment of the advance fixed by the Court, ensures that the Court remains in charge of determining the amount of the advances on costs. In some cases, the Secretariat may determine that it is not necessary or appropriate to fix a provisional advance and the Court's determination under Article 30(3) will be the only determination of an advance on costs.

The omission of the provision of Article 14 of the 1980 Internal Rules, that where the Court has fixed separate advances the parties may nevertheless agree to pay them in equal shares, corresponds to practice. The fixing of separate advances is almost always at the demand of a party for the express purpose of securing inequality of advances. Despite the omission of the clause, nothing would prevent the parties from agreeing amongst themselves to such an arrangement and requesting the court to accept such an agreement. However, this is an unlikely scenario.

OTHER REFERENCES:

C.P. & P., Chapter 4, "Advance to Cover Costs".

The Court recommended that the following sentence be added after the second paragraph of Article 9(1):

> When the Court has fixed separate advances on costs, the Secretariat requests each of the parties to pay the amount corresponding to its claims, without prejudice to the right of the parties to pay the said advances on costs in equal shares, if they deem it advisable.

30(4) When a request for an advance on costs has not been complied with, and after consultation with the Arbitral Tribunal, the Secretary General may direct the Arbitral Tribunal to suspend its work and set a time limit, which must be not less than 15 days, on the expiry of which the relevant claims, or counterclaims shall be considered as withdrawn. Should the party in question wish to object to this measure it must make a request within the aforementioned period for the matter to be decided by the Court. Such party shall not be prevented on the ground of such withdrawal from reintroducing the same claims or counterclaims at a later date in another proceeding.

PRIOR TEXT: Article 15, 1980 Internal Rules, incorporating substance of Article 9(3), 1975 Rules

Article 9(3), 1975 Rules

The Secretariat may make the transmission of the file to the arbitrator conditional upon the payment by the parties or on of them of the whole or part of the advance on costs to the International Chamber of Commerce.

Article 9 (4), 1975 Rules

When the Terms of Reference are communicated to the Court in accordance with the provisions of Article 13, the Court shall verify whether the requests for the advance on costs have been complied with.

Article 15, 1980 Internal Rules

When a request for an advance on costs has not been complied with, the Secretariat may set a time-limit, which must not be less than 30 days, on the expiry of which the relevant claim, whether principal claim or counter-claim, shall be considered as withdrawn. This does not prevent the party in question from lodging a new claim at a later date.

Should one of the parties wish to object to this measure, he must make a request, within the aforementioned period, for the matter to be decided by the Court.

MODIFICATION: Article 15 of the 1980 Internal Rules has been incorporated into Article 30(4), 1998 Rules. The provision of Article 9(3), 1975 Rules that the Secretariat "may make the transmission of the file to the arbitrator conditional upon the payment "of the whole or part of the advance on costs" has been omitted to eliminate any automatic blocking of the transmission of the file because of the non-payment of advances on costs. The 1975 Rules' provision that the Secretariat may refuse to transmit the file to the Arbitral Tribunal because of non-payment of an advance is replaced by the Secretariat's power "after consultation with the Arbitral Tribunal" to "direct the Arbitral Tribunal to suspend its work". The time limit for payment after such a suspension is reduced from 30 to 15 days, after which the claim or counterclaim is considered withdrawn. Such withdrawal is without prejudice to resubmission at a later date but it is now stipulated that any such resubmission must be "in another proceeding".

COMMENT: Inclusion in the 1998 Rules of the relevant section of the prior Internal Rules is consistent with the revision policy. Under Article 9(3) of the 1975 Rules, and the Court's regulations thereunder (Article 2(b) of "Schedule of Conciliation and Arbitration costs in effect from January 1, 1993"), the transmission of the file to the Arbitral Tribunal was conditional on at least half of the advance on costs being paid, and the Terms of Reference would only come into effect when the totality of the advance on costs had been paid (Article 9(4), 1975 Rules). This disassociation of payment of the advance on costs from the transmission of the arbitration file and continuation of the proceedings is an important modification to the Rules which speeds up the arbitral process by removing any automatic suspension of the work of the Arbitral Tribunal due to a problem of payment of an advance on costs.

Past practice indicates that the time-limit which the Secretariat will fix for payment, after which the claim or counterclaim will be considered to be withdrawn, will only be given after discussion to determine whether there is any legitimate excuse for delay in payment. The new text adds that if a claim has been withdrawn for nonpayment it may be later reintroduced but only "in another proceeding". The dilatory party may not encumber the pending arbitration with the reintroduced claim

OTHER REFERENCES:

C.P. & P., Sec. 14.01 "Payment of advance as condition for entry into effect of the Terms of Reference".

The Court recommended that the following subsections be added to "Advances to Cover Costs of Arbitration":

When a request for an advance on costs has not been complied with, the Secretariat may set a time-limit, which must not be less than 30 days, on the expiry of which the relevant claim, whether principal claim or counter-claim, shall be considered as withdrawn. This does not prevent the party in question from lodging a new claim at a later date.

Should one of the parties wish to object to this measure, he must make a request, within the aforementioned period, for the matter to be decided by the Court.

30(5) If one of the parties claims a right to a set-off with regard to either claims or counterclaims, such set-off shall be taken into account in determining the advance to cover the costs of arbitration in the same way as a separate claim insofar as it may require the Arbitral Tribunal to consider additional matters.

PRIOR TEXT: Article 16, 1980 Internal Rules

Article 16

If one of the parties claims a right to a set-off with regard to either a principal claim or counter-claim, such set-off is taken into account in determining the advance to cover the costs of arbitration, in the same way as a separate claim, insofar as it may require the Arbitral Tribunal to consider additional matters.

MODIFICATION: "[S]hall be" replaces "is" in the revised article to conform with language used throughout the text of the 1998 Rules.

COMMENT: In past practice a party was sometimes surprised to discover that as a result of the application of Article 16 of the Court's prior Internal Rules, its plea of a defense by way of set-off had the effect of increasing the amount in dispute and thus the total advance on costs in the same way as if it had sought positive relief by way of a counterclaim. The incorporation into the 1998 Rules of the provision of the prior Internal Rules, consistent with the goals of the revision, provides more transparency for arbitration users. It remains within the discretion of the Court in fixing the advances, to determine whether under the circumstances the Arbitral Tribunal will be required "to consider additional matters". The tendency of past practice was to find that in most cases it would, and to increase the advance on costs on the basis of the amount of the claimed set-off.

For comment on when and in what form a set-off may be claimed, *see* Comment under Article 5(5), *supra*.

OTHER REFERENCES:

The Court recommended that the section, as written above, be incorporated into Article 9 of the 1975 Rules "Advances to Cover Costs of Arbitration".

Article 31
Decision as to the Costs of the Arbitration

31(1) The costs of the arbitration shall include the fees and expenses of the arbitrators and the ICC administrative costs fixed by the Court, in accordance with the scale in force at the time of the commencement of the arbitral proceedings, as well as the fees and expenses of any experts appointed by the Arbitral Tribunal and the reasonable legal and other costs incurred by the parties for the arbitration.

PRIOR TEXT: Article 20(2), 1975 Rules

Article 20(2)

The costs of the arbitration shall include the arbitrator's fees and the administrative costs fixed by the International Court of Arbitration in accordance with the scale annexed to the present Rules, the expenses, if any, of the arbitrator, the fees and expenses of any experts, and the normal legal costs incurred by the parties.

MODIFICATION: Abbreviations have been used in this subsection for those terms previously defined in the text. The scale of costs is now defined as "the scale in force at the time of commencement of the arbitral proceedings" rather than "the scale annexed to the present Rules". "[R]easonable" is used in place of "normal" in the last line. Terms have been more clearly defined.

COMMENT: A schedule of arbitration costs, containing a scale of costs based on the amount in dispute, is attached as Appendix III. The scale may be changed from time to time. The revision makes clear that the scale to be applied is, consistent with the Court's longstanding practice, the scale in force on the date of receipt of the Request for Arbitration.

Reasonable legal costs incurred by the parties for the arbitration do not ordinarily include legal costs incurred in judicial proceedings ancillary to the arbitration. For an Award in which the Arbitral Tribunal declined to award such costs, *see* Case N° 6268 (1990) 3 ICC Collection, 68.

OTHER REFERENCES:

C.P. & P., Chapter 21 "Determination of Costs".

The Court recommended the following sentence be added:

> The applicable scales of administrative expenses and arbitrator's fees shall be those in force on the date of receipt of the Request for Arbitration by the Secretariat.

The Court further commented:

This provision was intended to eliminate uncertainties that may arise when the scales are revised. This is in accordance with practice since 1975.

See E. Schwartz, "The ICC Arbitral Process, Part IV: The Costs of ICC Arbitration", 4 *ICC Bull.* No. 1, 8 (1993).

31(2) The Court may fix the fees of the arbitrators at a figure higher or lower than that which would result from the application of the relevant scale should this be deemed necessary due to the exceptional circumstances of the case. Decisions on costs other than those fixed by the Court may be taken by the Arbitral Tribunal at any time during the proceedings.

PRIOR TEXT: Article 20(3), 1975 Rules

The Court may fix the arbitrator's fees at a figure higher or lower than that which would result from the application of the annexed scale if in the exceptional circumstances of the case this appears to be necessary.

MODIFICATION: "Relevant scale" is used in place of "annexed scale". Some terms are now defined more clearly.

COMMENT: Costs fixed by the Court and included in the final award are the fees and expenses of the arbitrators and the ICC administrative costs (*see* Article 31(1). Other costs which may be determined by the Arbitral Tribunal at any time include, for instance, costs of a neutral expert appointed by the Tribunal and other measures providing evidence and testimony. The power of the Arbitral Tribunal to take decisions on costs at any time during the proceedings helps to discourage the parties from making frivolous demands.

OTHER REFERENCES:

C.P.&P., Section 21.03, "Arbitrators' Fees".

31(3) The final Award shall fix the costs of the arbitration and decide which of the parties shall bear them or in what proportion they shall be borne by the parties.

PRIOR TEXT: Article 20(1), 1975 Rules

Article 20(1)

The arbitrator's award shall, in addition to dealing with the merits of the case, fix the costs of the arbitration and decide which of the parties shall bear the costs or in what proportions the costs shall be borne by the parties.

MODIFICATION: The defining word "final" is placed before "award", and "arbitrator's" is omitted. The phrase "in addition to dealing with the merits of the case" is omitted. Some grammatical changes have been made.

COMMENT: The word "final" is added to emphasize that ordinarily the costs of the arbitration should only be fixed in the final award made by the tribunal, meaning in this context, the last award which it will render. Arbitration costs will not be fixed in interim and partial awards even though such awards may be "final" and enforceable as to the issues they resolve.

OTHER REFERENCES:

MISCELLANEOUS

Article 32
Modified Time Limits

32(1) The parties may agree to shorten the various time limits set out in these Rules. Any such agreement entered into subsequent to the constitution of an Arbitral Tribunal shall become effective only upon the approval of the Arbitral Tribunal.

PRIOR TEXT: NEW

MODIFICATION: N.A.

COMMENT: This new article responds to the criticism of delay in the arbitral process and manifests the Court's willingness to supervise and administer arbitrations under ICC Rules under such shortened time-tables as the parties may agree. It was not thought desirable to attempt to provide a detailed fast-track regime to be adopted in arbitration agreements in advance. Although the general provision does not prevent parties from establishing detailed fast-track provisions in arbitration clauses, the limited experience of the ICC with this regime indicates that in most cases it will only be after the dispute has arisen that it will be practical to determine whether the parties are willing to cooperate to obtain an expedited award, requiring the waiver of various time limits designed for the protection of the parties. Moreover, the procedure to be adopted for a fast-track regime will vary with the circumstances of the case.

The provision of Article 32(2) that the Court may extend, under the prescribed circumstances, party-agreed time limits preserves the sanctity of the arbitral process and may be required to protect parties from unexpected consequences of their own agreement. The general rule, however, consistent with other modifications of the Rules, is to give the parties wide freedom to tailor the details of the arbitration procedure by means of their agreement.

It should be noted that while the Court has a reserved power to extend party-agreed fast-track time limits, for the purposes set out in the Rule, the Arbitral Tribunal does not. Where a time limit previously agreed to by the parties causes an important procedural problem, perhaps even frustration of the arbitral process, the Arbitral Tribunal may attempt to lead the parties to a revised agreement. But in the event that one party does not agree, the sole way of obtaining an extension would appear to be for the Arbitral Tribunal to bring the matter to the attention of the Court.

OTHER REFERENCES:

This rule follows the example of the WIPO Rules, which offers expedited arbitration rules. The WIPO Rules include a separate version for the purpose of expediting the arbitration procedure. The WIPO Expedited Arbitration Rules, effective from October 1, 1994, set out the following summary of such fast-track arbitration:

Summary

The WIPO Expedited Arbitration Rules consist of the WIPO Arbitration Rules modified in certain respects in order to ensure that the arbitration can be conducted in a shortened time frame and at reduced cost. To achieve these objectives, four main modifications have been introduced into the WIPO Arbitration Rules:

    i. The Statement of claim must accompany (and not be filed later and separately from) the Request for Arbitration. Similarly, the Statement of Defense must accompany the Answer to the Request.

    ii. There is always a sole arbitrator.

    iii. Any hearings before the sole arbitrator are condensed and may not, save in exceptional circumstance, exceed three days.

    iv. The time limits applying to the various stages of arbitral proceedings have been shortened. In particular, the proceedings should, whenever reasonably possible, be declared closed within three months (as opposed to nine months under the WIPO Arbitration Rules) of either the delivery of the Statement of Defense or the establishment of the Tribunal, whichever event occurs later, and the final award should, whenever reasonably possible, be made within one month (as opposed to three months under the WIPO Arbitration Rules) thereafter .

See ICC Arbitration Nos. 7385 and 7402 of 1992, 18 *Yearbook* 68 (1992) (finding that party-agreed shortened time limits establishing a fast track arbitration did not conflict with the 1975 Rules).

See B. Davis; P. Nickles and M. Silverman; D. Watkiss; H. Smit , "ICC Fast Track Arbitration: Different Perspectives", 3 *ICC Bull.* No. 2, p. 4 (1992).

See "Special Section: Fast Track Arbitration", 2 *The American Review of International Arbitration*, N° 2 (1991).

    These two compilations of articles, based on ICC Arbitrations Nos. 7385 and 7402, follow a complex price determination case from the Request for Arbitration to the Award from the perspectives of the ICC Court, counsel for the parties and the Chairman of the Arbitral Tribunal. This case represents an example of a fast track arbitration which worked to the general satisfaction of the parties and is a useful case study.

See M. Silverman, "The Fast Track Arbitration of the International Chamber of Commerce — The User's Point of View", 10 *J. Int'l Arb.* No. 4, p. 113 (1993).

See M. Mustill, "Comments on Fast-Track Arbitration" 10 *J. Int'l Arb.* No. 4, p. 121 (1993).

32(2) The Court, on its own initiative, may extend any time limit which has been modified pursuant to Article 32(1) if it decides that it is necessary to do so in order that the Arbitral Tribunal or the Court may fulfil their responsibilities in accordance with these Rules.

PRIOR TEXT: NEW

MODIFICATIONS: N.A.

COMMENT: *See* Comment at Article 32(1).

OTHER REFERENCES: *See* Other References at Article 32(1).

Article 33
Waiver

A party which proceeds with the arbitration without raising its objection to a failure to comply with any provisions of these Rules, or of any other rules applicable to the proceedings, any direction given by the Arbitral Tribunal, or any requirement under the arbitration agreement relating to the constitution of the Arbitral Tribunal, or to the conduct of the proceedings, shall be deemed to have waived its right to object.

PRIOR TEXT: NEW

MODIFICATION: N.A.

COMMENT: This section reflects the need to prevent a party from raising untimely objections (frequently late in a case when an unfavorable outcome of the arbitration appears to be likely) to arbitrators' conduct of the proceedings if they have not made objections in the course thereof. Stipulations to this effect are set out in many other arbitration rules as well as the UNCITRAL Model Law. Consistent with the general drafting of the Rules, not all the details of applicability of the waiver clause are spelled out. It is not indicated within what time period objections must be raised or in what form, as is the case in some other rules. These matters are within the discretion of the Arbitral Tribunal subject only to possible review by national courts in enforcement or judicial recourse proceedings.

OTHER REFERENCES:

UNCITRAL Rules, Article 30:

> A party who knows that any provision of, or requirement under, these Rules has not been complied with and yet proceeds with the arbitration without promptly stating his objection to such non-compliance, shall be deemed to have waived his right to object.

UNCITRAL Model Law, Article 4:

> A party who knows that any provisions of this Law from which the parties may derogate or any requirement under the arbitration agreement has not been complied with and yet proceeds with the arbitration without stating his objection to such non-compliance without delay or, if a time-limit is provided therefor, within such period of time, shall be deemed to have waived his right to object.

LCIA Rules, Article 20.1:

> A party who knows that any provision of, or requirement under, these Rules has not been complied with and yet proceeds with the arbitration without

promptly stating his objection to such non-compliance, shall be deemed to have waived its right to object.

AAA International Rules, Article 25:

A party who knows that any provision of the rules or requirement under the rules has not been complied with, but proceeds with the arbitration without promptly stating an objection in writing thereto, shall be deemed to have waived the right to object.

Stockholm Rules, Article 24:

A party who fails during the proceedings to object within a reasonable time to any deviation from provisions of the arbitration agreement or other rules applicable to the proceedings shall be deemed to have waived his right to invoke such irregularity.

WIPO Rules, Article 58:

A party which knows that any provision of, or requirement under, these Rules, or any direction given by the Tribunal, has not been complied with, and yet proceeds with the arbitration without promptly recording an objection to such non-compliance shall be deemed to have waived its right to object.

Article 34
Exclusion of liability

Neither the arbitrators, nor the Court and its members, nor the ICC and its employees, nor the ICC National Committees shall be liable to any person for any act or omission in connection with the arbitration.

PRIOR TEXT: NEW

MODIFICATION: N.A.

COMMENT: The addition of this article is consistent with the arbitration rules of other international institutions and provides some protection for arbitrators and other participants in the administration of ICC arbitration. As a rule agreed by the parties having accepted ICC arbitration, it binds the parties contractually. Stated in terms of an absolute exclusion of liability, its effectiveness may be limited by mandatory terms of applicable law, the provision of such laws varying widely from jurisdiction to jurisdiction. The clause should nevertheless have a salutary effect in deterring claims against arbitrators or the arbitral institution (compare the terms of Article 28(6)) regarding the parties' obligations concerning the enforceability of awards as to which the parties "shall be deemed to have waived their right to any form of recourse insofar as such waiver can be validly made").

The Working Party of the Arbitration Commission had initially proposed that any "deliberate wrong doing" be excluded from the arbitrator's exemption (Draft of 27 September 1996, ICC Doc. No. 420/15-015), to which had been added "or gross negligence" (ICC Doc. No. 420/357 of 13 January 1997). However, after receipt of comments from National Committees indicating concern that the new rule might expand rather than restrict arbitrator liability (said to be excluded absolutely under some national laws) the draft recommended by the Working Party and approved by the Arbitration Commission provided for absolute exclusion of liability. The ICC Court had opposed the exclusion of liability clause as recommended by the Arbitration Commission partially because of its absolute terms and partially because of its extension to the ICC Court and others with an administrative role who could not be considered to fall within the quasi-judicial function, and corresponding immunity, of arbitrators. The Court's position would seem to be at odds with the practice of other arbitral institutions which have attempted in their rules (*see* "Other References" below) to extend immunity to cover the administrative acts of the arbitral institution. The English Arbitration Act 1996 (Section 74) has specifically extended to arbitral institutions immunity from any liability flowing from the appointment of arbitrators. Some national courts have on their own initiative extended immunity to cover institutional actions which are indispensable to the arbitral proceedings. *See* Corbin v. Washington Fire & Marine Insurance Co., 278 F. Supp. 393 (D.S.C. 1968), app'd 398 F. 2d 543 (4th Cir. 1968). The ICC Council at its April 27, 1997 meeting in Shanghaï approved the absolute immunity text of the article, recognizing that in some jurisdictions at least mandatory provisions of national law might provide more restricted immunity.

OTHER REFERENCES:

AAA International Rules, Article 35 "Exclusion of Liability"

> The members of the tribunal and the administrator shall not be liable to any party for any act or omission in connection with any arbitration conducted under these rules, except that they may be liable for the consequences of conscious and deliberate wrongdoing.

WIPO Rules, Article 77 "Exclusion of Liability"

> Except in respect of deliberate wrongdoing, the arbitrator or arbitrators, WIPO and the Center shall not be liable to a party for any act or omission in connection with the arbitration.

LCIA Rules, Article 19 "Exclusion of Liability"

> 19.1 Neither the Court nor any arbitrator shall be liable to any party for any act or omission in connection with any arbitration conducted under these Rules, save that arbitrators (but not the Court) may be liable for the consequences of conscious and deliberate wrongdoing.

See E. Robine, "The Liability of Arbitrators and Arbitral Institutions in International Arbitrations under French Law", 5 *Arb. Int'l* 323 (1989).

See J.D.M. Lew, "The Immunity of Arbitrators", Lloyd's of London Press, London, 1990.

Article 35
General Rule

In all matters not expressly provided for in these Rules, the Court and the Arbitral Tribunal shall act in the spirit of these Rules and shall make every effort to make sure that the Award is enforceable at law.

PRIOR TEXT: Article 26, 1975 Rules

Article 26

In all matters not expressly provided for in these Rules, the International Court of Arbitration and the arbitrator shall act in the spirit of these Rules and shall make every effort to make sure that the award is enforceable at law.

MODIFICATION: The term "arbitrator" is replaced by "Arbitral Tribunal". The term "International Court of Arbitration" is shortened to "Court".

COMMENT: The modifications made are consistent with those found throughout the 1998 Rules.

OTHER REFERENCES:

CONVERSION TABLES

(A) Destination table: from 1975 Arbitration Rules to 1998 Arbitration Rules

(B) Derivative table: from 1998 Arbitration Rules to 1975 Arbitration Rules

(C) Destination table: from 1980 Internal Rules* to 1998 Internal Rules

(D) Derivative table: from 1998 Internal Rules to 1980 Internal Rules*

*Refe rence is to Internal Rules first adopted in 1980 as amended and in effect on January 1, 1988.

Destination table: From 1975 Arbitration Rules to 1998 Arbitration Rules

Table A

TABLE A	
From: 1975 ARBITRATION RULES	**To: 1998 ARBITRATION RULES**
ARTICLE 1: INTERNATIONAL COURT OF ARBITRATION	
Article 1(1)	Article 1(1)
Article 1(2)	Article 1(2)
Article 1(3)	Article 1(3)
Article 1(4)	Article 1(4)
Article 1(5)	Article 1(5)
ARTICLE 2: THE ARBITRAL TRIBUNAL	
Article 2(1)	Article 1(2); Article 7(6); Article 9(1)
Article 2(2)	Article 2(i); Article 8(1)
Article 2(3)	Article 8(3)
Article 2(4)	Article 8(4)
Article 2(5)	Article 8(2)
Article 2(6)	Article 9(3); Article 9(4); Article 9(5); Article 9(6)
Article 2(7)	Article 7(1); Article 7(2); Article 7(3)
Article 2(8)	Article 11(1); Article 11(2)
Article 2(9)	Article 11(3)

TABLE A	
From: 1975 ARBITRATION RULES	**To: 1998 ARBITRATION RULES**
Article 2(10)	Article 12(1)
Article 2(11)	Article 12(2); Article 12(3)
Article 2(12)	Article 12(4)
Article 2(13)	Article 7(4)
ARTICLE 3: REQUEST FOR ARBITRATION	
Article 3(1)	Article 4(1); Article 4(2)
Article 3(2)	Article 4(3)
Article 3(3)	Article 4(5)
ARTICLE 4: ANSWER TO THE REQUEST	
Article 4(1)	Article 5(1); Article 5(2)
Article 4(2)	Article 5(4)
ARTICLE 5: COUNTER-CLAIM	
Article 5(1)	Article 5(5)
Article 5(2)	Article 5(6)
ARTICLE 6: PLEADINGS AND WRITTEN STATEMENTS, NOTIFICATIONS OR COMMUNICATIONS	
Article 6(1)	Article 3(1)
Article 6(2)	Article 3(2)
Article 6(3)	Article 3(3)
Article 6(4)	Article 3(4)

TABLE A	
From: 1975 ARBITRATION RULES	**To: 1998 ARBITRATION RULES**
ARTICLE 7: ABSENCE OF AGREEEMENT TO ARBITRATE	
Article 7	Article 6(2)
ARTICLE 8: EFFECT OF THE AGREEMENT TO ARBITRATE	
Article 8(1)	Article 6(1)
Article 8(2)	Article 6(3)
Article 8(3)	Article 6(2)
Article 8(4)	Article 6(4)
Article 8(5)	Article 23(2)
ARTICLE 9: ADVANCE TO COVER COSTS OF ARBITRATION	
Article 9(1)	Article 30(2)
Article 9(2)	Article 30(3)
Article 9(3)	Article 13; Article 30(4)
Article 9(4)	Article 30(4)
ARTICLE 10: TRANSMISSION OF THE FILE TO THE ARBITRATOR	
Article 10	Article 13
ARTICLE 11: RULES GOVERNING THE PROCEEDIINGS	
Article 11	Article 15(1)
ARTICLE 12: PLACE OF ARBITRATION	
Article 12	Article 14(1)

TABLE A	
From: 1975 ARBITRATION RULES	**To: 1998 ARBITRATION RULES**
ARTICLE 13: TERMS OF REFERENCE	
Article 13(1)	Article 18(1)
Article 13(2)	Article 18(2); Article 18(3)
Article 13(3)	Article 17(1)
Article 13(4)	Article 17(3)
Article 13(5)	Article 17(2)
ARTICLE 14: THE ARBITRAL PROCEEDINGS	
Article 14(1)	Article 20(1); Article 20(2); Article 20(3)
Article 14(2)	Article 20(4)
Article 14(3)	Article 20(6)
ARTICLE 15	
Article 15(1)	Article 21(1)
Article 15(2)	Article 21(2)
Article 15(3)	Article 16
Article 15(4)	Article 21(3)
Article 15(5)	Article 21(4)
ARTICLE 16	
Article 16	Article 19
ARTICLE 17: AWARD BY CONSENT	
Article 17	Article 26

TABLE A	
From: 1975 ARBITRATION RULES	**To: 1998 ARBITRATION RULES**
ARTICLE 18: TIME-LIMIT FOR AWARD	
Article 18(1)	Article 24(1)
Article 18(2)	Article 24(2)
Article 18(3)	N.A.
ARTICLE 19: AWARD BY THREE ARBITRATORS	
Article 19	Article 25(1)
ARTICLE 20: DECISION AS TO COSTS OF ARBITRATION	
Article 20(1)	Article 31(3)
Article 20(2)	Article 31(1)
Article 20(3)	Article 31(2)
ARTICLE 21: SCRUTINY OF AWARD BY THE COURT	
Article 21	Article 27
ARTICLE 22: MAKING OF AWARD	
Article 22	Article 25(3)
ARTICLE 23: NOTIFICATION OF AWARD TO PARTIES	
Article 23(1)	Article 28(1)
Article 23(2)	Article 28(2)
Article 23(3)	Article 28(3)
ARTICLE 24: FINALITY AND ENFORCEABILITY OF AWARD	
Article 24(1)	Article 28(6)
Article 24(2)	Article 28(6)

TABLE A	
From: 1975 ARBITRATION RULES	**To: 1998 ARBITRATION RULES**
ARTICLE 25: DEPOSIT OF AWARD	
Article 25	Article 28(4); Article 28(5)
ARTICLE 26: GENERAL RULE	
Article 26	Article 35

Derivative table: from 1998 Arbitration Rules to 1975 Arbitration Rules

Table B

TABLE B	
From: 1998 ARBITRATION RULES	**To: 1975 ARBITRATION RULES**
INTRODUCTORY PROVISIONS	
ARTICLE 1: INTERNATIONAL COURT OF ARBITRATION	
Article 1(1)	Article 1(1); Article 1, Internal Rules
Article 1(2)	Article 2(1); Article 1(2)
Article 1(3)	Article 1(3)
Article 1(4)	Article 1(4)
Article 1(5)	Article 1(5)
ARTICLE 2: DEFINITIONS	
Article 2(i)	Article 2(2)
Article 2(ii)	NEW
Article 2(iii)	NEW
ARTICLE 3: WRITTEN NOTIFICATIONS OR COMMUNICATIONS; TIME LIMITS	
Article 3(1)	Article 6(1); NEW
Article 3(2)	Article 6(2)
Article 3(3)	Article 6(3)
Article 3(4)	Article 6(4)

TABLE B	
From: 1998 ARBITRATION RULES	**To: 1975 ARBITRATION RULES**
COMMENCING THE ARBITRATION	
ARTICLE 4: REQUEST FOR ARBITRATION	
Article 4(1)	Article 3(1)
Article 4(2)	Article 3(1)
Article 4(3)	Article 3(2)
Article 4(4)	NEW
Article 4(5)	Article 3(3)
Article 4(6)	Article 13, Internal Rules
ARTICLE 5: ANSWER TO THE REQUEST; COUNTERCLAIMS	
Article 5(1)	Article 4(1)
Article 5(2)	Article 4(1)
Article 5(3)	NEW
Article 5(4)	Article 4(2)
Article 5(5)	Article 5(1)
Article 5(6)	Article 5(2)
ARTICLE 6: EFFECT OF THE ARBITRATION AGREEMENT	
Article 6(1)	Article 8(1)
Article 6(2)	Article 8(3); Article 7; Article 12, Internal Rules
Article 6(3)	Article 8(2)
Article 6(4)	Article 8(4)

TABLE B	
From: 1998 ARBITRATION RULES	**To: 1975 ARBITRATION RULES**
THE ARBITRAL TRIBUNAL	
ARTICLE 7: GENERAL PROVISIONS	
Article 7(1)	Article 2(7)
Article 7(2)	Article 2(7)
Article 7(3)	Article 2(7)
Article 7(4)	Article 2(13)
Article 7(5)	NEW
Article 7(6)	Article 2(1)
ARTICLE 8: NUMBER OF ARBITRATORS	
Article 8(1)	Article 2(2)
Article 8(2)	Article 2(5)
Article 8(3)	Article 2(3)
Article 8(4)	Article 2(4)
ARTICLE 9: APPOINTMENT AND CONFIRMATION OF THE ARBITRATORS	
Article 9(1)	Article 2(1)
Article 9(2)	NEW
Article 9(3)	Article 2(6)
Article 9(4)	Article 2(6)
Article 9(5)	Article 2(6)
Article 9(6)	Article 2(6)

TABLE B	
From: 1998 ARBITRATION RULES	**To: 1975 ARBITRATION RULES**
ARTICLE 10: MULTIPLE PARTIES	
Article 10(1)	NEW
Article 10(2)	NEW
ARTICLE 11: CHALLENGE OF ARBITRATORS	
Article 11(1)	Article 2(8)
Article 11(2)	Article 2(8)
Article 11(3)	Article 2(9)
ARTICLE 12: REPLACEMENT OF ARBITRATORS	
Article 12(1)	Article 2(10)
Article 12(2)	Article 2(11)
Article 12(3)	Article 2(11)
Article 12(4)	Article 2(12)
Article 12(5)	NEW
THE ARBITRAL PROCEEDINGS	
ARTICLE 13: TRANSMISSION OF THE FILE TO THE ARBITRAL TRIBUNAL	
Article 13	Article 9(3); Article 10
ARTICLE 14: PLACE OF THE ARBITRATION	
Article 14(1)	Article 12
Article 14(2)	NEW
Article 14(3)	NEW

TABLE B	
From: 1998 ARBITRATION RULES	**To: 1975 ARBITRATION RULES**
ARTICLE 15: RULES GOVERNING THE PROCEEDINGS	
Article 15(1)	Article 11
Article 15(2)	NEW
ARTICLE 16: LANGUAGE OF THE ARBITRATION	
Article 16	Article 15(3)
ARTICLE 17: APPLICABLE RULES OF LAW	
Article 17(1)	Article 13(3)
Article 17(2)	Article 13(5)
Article 17(3)	Article 13(4)
ARTICLE 18: TERMS OF REFERENCE; PROCEDURAL TIMETABLE	
Article 18(1)	Article 13(1)
Article 18(2)	Article 13(2)
Article 18(3)	Article 13(2)
Article 18(4)	NEW
ARTICLE 19: NEW CLAIMS	
Article 19	Article 16
ARTICLE 20: ESTABLISHING THE FACTS OF THE CASE	
Article 20(1)	Article 14(1)
Article 20(2)	Article 14(1)
Article 20(3)	Article 14(1)
Article 20(4)	Article 14(2)

TABLE B	
From: 1998 ARBITRATION RULES	**To: 1975 ARBITRATION RULES**
Article 20(5)	NEW
Article 20(6)	Article 14(3)
Article 20(7)	NEW
ARTICLE 21: HEARINGS	
Article 21(1)	Article 15(1)
Article 21(2)	Article 15(2)
Article 21(3)	Article 15(4)
Article 21(4)	Article 15(5)
ARTICLE 22: CLOSING OF THE PROCEEDINGS	
Article 22(1)	NEW
Article 22(2)	NEW
ARTICLE 23: CONSERVATORY AND INTERIM MEASURES	
Article 23(1)	NEW
Article 23(2)	NEW; Article 8(5)
AWARDS	
ARTICLE 24: TIME LIMIT FOR THE AWARD	
Article 24(1)	Article 18(1)
Article 24(2)	Article 18(2)
ARTICLE 25: MAKING OF THE AWARD	
Article 25(1)	Article 19
Article 25(2)	NEW

TABLE B	
From: 1998 ARBITRATION RULES	**To: 1975 ARBITRATION RULES**
Article 25(3)	Article 22
ARTICLE 26: AWARD BY CONSENT	
Article 26	Article 17
ARTICLE 27: SCRUTINY OF THE AWARD BY THE COURT	
Article 27	Article 21
ARTICLE 28: NOTIFICATION, DEPOSIT AND ENFORCEABILITY OF THE AWARD	
Article 28(1)	Article 23(1)
Article 28(2)	Article 23(2)
Article 28(3)	Article 23(3)
Article 28(4)	Article 25
Article 28(5)	Article 25
Article 28(6)	Article 24(1); Article 24(2)
ARTICLE 29: CORRECTION AND INTERPRETATION OF THE AWARD	
Article 29(1)	NEW
Article 29(2)	NEW
Article 29(3)	NEW
COSTS	
ARTICLE 30: ADVANCE TO COVER THE COSTS OF THE ARBITRATION	
Article 30(1)	NEW
Article 30(2)	Article 9(1)

TABLE B	
From: 1998 ARBITRATION RULES	**To: 1975 ARBITRATION RULES**
Article 30(3)	Article 9(2); Article 14, Internal Rules
Article 30(4)	Article 9(3); Article 15, Internal Rules
Article 30(5)	Article 16, Internal Rules
ARTICLE 31: DECISION AS TO THE COSTS OF THE ARBITRATION	
Article 31(1)	Article 20(2)
Article 31(2)	Article 20(3)
Article 31(3)	Article 20(1)
MISCELLANEOUS	
ARTICLE 32: MODIFIED TIME LIMITS	
Article 32(1)	NEW
Article 32(2)	NEW
ARTICLE 33: WAIVER	
Article 33	NEW
ARTICLE 34: EXCLUSION OF LIABILITY	
Article 34	NEW
ARTICLE 35: GENERAL RULE	
Article 35	Article 26

Table C

**Destination table:
from 1980 Internal Rules* to 1998 Internal Rules**

Table C

TABLE C	
From: 1980 INTERNAL RULES	**To: 1998 ARBITRATION RULES, STATUTES, INTERNAL RULES, ARBITRATION COSTS AND FEES**
Article 1	Article 1(1), ICC Arbitration Rules
Article 2	Appendix I— Statutes, Article 6
Article 3	Article 1(1) and 1(2), Internal Rules
Article 4	Article 1(3), 1(4), 1(5), Internal Rules
Article 5	Article 2(1), 2(2), Internal Rules
Article 6	Article 2(3), 2(4), 2(5), Internal Rules
Article 7	Article 3(1), 3(2), Internal Rules
Article 8	Article 4(1), Internal Rules
Article 9	Article 4(2), 4(3), Internal Rules
Article 10	Article 4(4), Internal Rules
Article 11	Article 4(5), Internal Rules
Article 12	Article 6(3), Article 6(2), ICC Arbitration Rules
Article 13	Article 4(6), ICC Arbitration Rules
Article 14	Article 30(3), ICC Arbitration Rules
Article 15	Article 30(4), ICC Arbitration Rules

Table C

TABLE C	
From: 1980 INTERNAL RULES	**To: 1998 ARBITRATION RULES, STATUTES, INTERNAL RULES, ARBITRATION COSTS AND FEES**
Article 16	Article 30(5), ICC Arbitration Rules
Article 17	Article 6, Internal Rules
Article 18	Appendix III Arbitration Costs and Fees Article 2(2)

**Derivative table:
from 1998 Internal Rules to 1980 Internal Rules**

Table D

TABLE D	
1998 INTERNAL RULES	**1980 INTERNAL RULES**
Article 1(1)	Article 3
Article 1(2)	Article 3
Article 1(3)	Article 4
Article 1(4)	Article 4
Article 1(5)	Article 4
Article 1(6)	NEW
Article 1(7)	NEW
Article 2(1)	Article 5
Article 2(2)	Article 5
Article 2(3)	Article 6
Article 2(4)	Article 6
Article 2(5)	Article 6
Article 3(1)	Article 7
Article 3(2)	Article 7
Article 4(1)	Article 8
Article 4(2)	Article 9
Article 4(3)	Article 9

Article 4(4)	Article 10
Article 4(5)	Article 11
Article 5	NEW
Article 6	Article 17

APPENDICES

NOTE

The appendices set out below to the 1998 Arbitration Rules are effective as of January 1, 1998. The modifications were for the most part made in order to conform to the new Rules, and do not constitute any major change in and of themselves.

Appendix I: Statutes of the International Court of Arbitration of the ICC

The Statutes were last revised as of June 16, 1993. The Articles modified in 1998 include:

Article 4: Plenary Session of the Court (adding to the provisions for deliberations and quorum a provision concerning the presiding officer)

Article 5: Committees (gives a statutory basis for the provisions in the Rules and Internal Rules concerning committees)

Article 6: Confidentiality (gives a statutory basis for the provisions in the Rules and Internal Rules concerning confidentiality)

Article 7: Modification of the Rules of Arbitration (revising slightly the provisions concerning the roles of the Court and the ICC Commission on International Arbitration in proposing modifications to the Rules)

Appendix II — Internal Rules of the International Court of Arbitration

The Internal Rules were last revised in 1988. One of the purposes of the 1998 revision of the 1975 Arbitration Rules was to incorporate pertinent provisions of the Internal Rules. Thus the Internal Rules appear much changed but are in fact not so since the absent provisions now appear in the Arbitration Rules. It is important to note, however, that several changes have been made to the Internal Rules alone which may have an impact, albeit minimal, on the conduct of arbitrations commencing after January 1, 1998.

The Court has decided that the new Internal Rules set out in Appendix II apply as of January 1, 1998 to previously pending arbitrations, as well as to arbitrations commenced after January 1, 1998 to which the parties have agreed that the old Arbitration Rules will apply. However; in these cases articles 12 through 18 of the old Internal Rules will apply as well.

New or modified Articles of the 1998 Internal Rules include:

Article 1(6),1(7): These article subsections are new, and contain provisions governing the ICC's receipt of arbitration related correspondence and pleadings, and its custodianship thereof. *See* Comment at Article 3(1), 1998 Rules.

Article 2(2): The article has been modified to allow the Vice Chairmen, in addition to the members of the Court, to be proposed as an arbitrator by one or more of the parties, or pursuant to a procedure agreed by the parties. *See* Comment at Article 1(3), 1998 Rules.

Article 4(5): The modified article, which provides that the Court shall determine the decisions that may be taken by the Committee, no longer sets out the formal restriction that the Committee of the Court may not act on challenges of arbitrators or concerning allegations that an arbitrator is not fulfilling his functions, or the approval of draft awards. However, the Court has determined that ordinarily questions on the status of an arbitrator (challenges under Article 11(3), replacement of an arbitrator under Article 12(2) (4) for not fulfilling his duties, decisions not to replace an arbitrator subsequent to the closing of proceedings under Article 12(5)), will be decided by the Court in Plenary Session. On the other hand, the Court has determined that the Committee will be empowered to scrutinize arbitral awards, thus enabling the awards to be notified more rapidly to the parties. Awards which raise particular difficulties will continue to be reviewed and approved at a Plenary Session. *See* R. Briner; "The Implementation of the 1998 ICC Rules", 8 *ICC Bull.* No. 2, 7 (1997).

Article 6: The modification made to this article allows the Court to avoid being constrained by formalistic procedural requirements. It now states that the Court, in its scrutiny of draft awards, must consider the requirements of mandatory law at the place of arbitration, but only "to the extent practicable". *See* Comment at Article 27, 1998 Rules.

Prior Article 10, providing for the Secretariat, *sua sponte*, to draw the parties' attention to the fact that in the Secretariat's opinion there did not exist *prima facie* an arbitration agreement, has been eliminated. *See* Comment at Article 6(2), 1998 Rules.

Appendix III — Arbitration Costs and Fees

The schedule of arbitration costs and fees was last revised as of January 1, 1993.

The new schedule, according to its Article 4 (1), applies to all arbitrations commenced on or after January 1, 1998, including arbitrations which, by special agreement, are to be conducted under prior versions of the Rules.

The principal modifications of the 1998 schedule are:

Article 1: The new schedule conveniently separates the provisions for advances on costs (Article 1) and costs and fees (Article 2), the latter addressing the final determination of costs by the Court at the end of the arbitration. The lengthy Article 1 generally restates prior practice concerning the modalities of advance payment (*i.e.* when payments must be made "in cash," when bank guarantees are acceptable, the consequence of non payment, etc.). It has the advantage of gathering in one place the administrative rules which had previously been the subject of letters and circulars.

Article 1(1): The advance payment on ICC administrative expenses to accompany the request for arbitration is increased from $ 2,000 to $ 2,500.

Article 1(2): A formula is set out for the calculation of the new provisional advance on costs to be established by the Secretary General. *See* Article 30(1), 1998 Arbitration Rules.

Article 2(2): The Court in determining the arbitrator's fees is to take into account not only, as in the past, the time spent, the rapidity of the proceedings and the complexity of the dispute, but also the diligence of the arbitrator.

Article 2(6): The Court shall fix the costs of arbitration at its discretion when the arbitration terminates prior to the rendering of a final award.

Article 2(7): The Court may fix an additional advance on costs in the case of an application for correction or interpretation of an award under Article 29(2) of the 1998 Rules.

Article 2(9): Article 2(9) confirms the prior practice that arbitration costs and fees assessed by the Court and included in the Award do not include any provision for taxes payable by the arbitrators and notably the Value Added Tax (VAT) to which many arbitrators are subject. Parties are expected to pay such charges but "recovery of any such charges or taxes is a matter solely between the arbitrator and the parties". The obligation of arbitrators established in the European Union to pay value added taxes on arbitration fees has taken on a new dimension because of the controversial finding of the European Court of Justice in Bernd von Hoffman (Judgment of 16 September 1997) that arbitrators' fees, unlike those of lawyers, consultants, engineers and accountants are subject to value added tax even on export transactions (*i.e.* where the seat of arbitration or the domicile of the party to the arbitration is in a country other than the domicile of the arbitrator).

Scale of Charges (the "Barème"): The percentage charge to be applied to the amount in dispute in determining the amounts of the ICC administrative expenses and for arbitrators' fees has been increased. Charges for administrative expenses have been increased by 25 to 35% for arbitrations involving disputes up to ten million dollars and 15 to 20% for arbitrations above this amount. The ceiling for administrative expenses has been raised from $ 65,500 to $ 75,800. Charges for arbitrators' fees have been increased by 25 to 40% for arbitrations up to ten million dollars and by 15 to 20% for arbitrations above this amount.

APPENDIX I
STATUTES OF THE INTERNATIONAL COURT
OF ARBITRATION OF THE ICC

Article 1
Function

1. The function of the International Court of Arbitration of the International Chamber of Commerce (the Court) is to ensure the application of the Rules of Arbitration and of the Rules of Conciliation of the International Chamber of Commerce and it has all the necessary powers for that purpose.

2. As an autonomous body, it carries out these functions in complete independence from the ICC and its organs.

3. Its members are independent from the ICC National Committees.

Article 2
Composition of the Court

The Court shall consist of a Chairman, Vice-Chairmen and members and alternate members (collectively designated as members). In its work it is assisted by its Secretariat (Secretariat of the Court).

Article 3
Appointment

1. The Chairman is elected by the ICC Council upon recommendation of the Executive Board of the ICC.

2. The ICC Council appoints the Vice-Chairmen of the Court from among the members of the Court or otherwise.

3. Its members are appointed by the ICC Council on the proposal of National Committees, one member for each Committee.

4. On the proposal of the Chairman of the Court, the Council may appoint alternate members.

5. The term of office of all members is three years. If a member is no longer in a position to exercise his functions, his successor is appointed by the Council for the remainder of the term.

Article 4
Plenary Session of the Court

The Plenary Sessions of the Court are presided over by the Chairman, or in his absence, by one of the Vice-Chairmen designated by him. The deliberations shall be valid when at least six members are present. Decisions are taken by a majority vote, the Chairman having a casting vote in the event of a tie.

Article 5
Committees

The Court may set up one or more Committees and lay down the functions and organization of such Committees.

Article 6
Confidentiality

The work of the Court is of a confidential nature and must be respected by everyone who participates in that work in whatever capacity. The Court lays down the rules regarding the persons who can attend the meetings of the Court and its Committees and who are entitled to have access to the materials submitted to the Court and its Secretariat.

Article 7
Modification of the Rules of Arbitration

Any proposal of the Court for a modification of the Rules is laid before the Commission on International Arbitration before submission to the Executive Board and the Council of the ICC for approval.

APPENDIX II
INTERNAL RULES OF THE INTERNATIONAL COURT OF
ARBITRATION OF THE ICC

Article 1
Confidential Character of the Work
of the International Court of Arbitration

1. The sessions of the Court, whether plenary or those of a Committee of the Court, are open only to its members and to the Secretariat.

2. However, in exceptional circumstances the Chairman of the Court may invite other persons to attend. Such persons must respect the confidential character of the work of the Court.

3. The documents submitted to the Court, or drawn up by it in the course of its proceedings, are communicated only to the members of the Court and to the Secretariat and to persons authorized by the Chairman to attend Court sessions.

4. The Chairman or the Secretary General of the Court may authorize researchers undertaking work of a scientific nature on international trade law to acquaint themselves with awards and other documents of general interest, with the exception of memoranda, notes, statements and documents remitted by the parties within the framework of arbitration proceedings.

5. Such authorization shall not be given unless the beneficiary has undertaken to respect the confidential character of the documents made available and to refrain from any publication in their respect without having previously submitted the text for approval to the Secretary General of the Court.

6. The Secretariat will in each case submitted to arbitration under the Rules retain in the archives of the Court all awards, terms of reference, decisions of the Court as well as copies of the pertinent correspondence of the Secretariat.

7. Any documents, communications or correspondence submitted by the parties or the arbitrators may be destroyed unless a party or an arbitrator requests in writing within a period fixed by the Secretariat the return of such documents. All related costs and expenses for the return of such documents shall be paid by such party or arbitrator.

Article 2
Participation of Members of the
International Court of Arbitration in ICC Arbitration

1. The Chairman and the members of the Secretariat of the Court may not act as arbitrators or as counsel in cases submitted to ICC arbitration.

2. The Court shall not appoint Vice-Chairmen or members of the Court as arbitrators. They may, however, be proposed for such duties by one or more of the parties, or pursuant to any other procedure agreed upon by the parties, subject to confirmation by the Court.

3. When the Chairman, a Vice-Chairman or a member of the Court or of the Secretariat is involved in any capacity whatsoever in proceedings pending before the Court, such person must inform the Secretary General of the Court upon becoming aware of such involvement.

4. Such person must refrain from participating in the discussions or in the decisions of the Court concerning the proceedings and must be absent from the courtroom whenever the matter is considered.

5. Such person will not receive any material documentation or information pertaining to such proceedings.

Article 3
Relations between the
Members of the Court and the
ICC National Committees

1. By virtue of their capacity, the members of the Court are independent of the ICC National Committees which proposed them for appointment by the ICC Council.

2. Furthermore, they must regard as confidential, vis-à-vis the said National Committees, any information concerning individual cases with which they have become acquainted in their capacity as members of the Court except when they have been requested by the Chairman of the Court, or by its Secretary General to communicate specific information to their respective National Committee.

Article 4
Committee of the Court

1. In accordance with the provisions of Article 1 (4) of the Rules and Article 5 of its Statutes (Appendix I), the Court hereby establishes a Committee of the Court.

2. The members of the Committee consist of a Chairman and at least two other members. The Chairman of the Court acts as the Chairman of the Committee. If absent, the Chairman may designate a Vice-Chairman of the Court or, in exceptional circumstances, another member of the Court as Chairman of the Committee.

3. The other two members of the Committee are appointed by the Court from among the Vice-Chairmen or the other members of the Court. At each Plenary Session the Court appoints the members who are to attend the meetings of the Committee to be held before the next Plenary Session.

4. The Committee meets when convened by its Chairman. Two members constitute a quorum.

5. (a) The Court shall determine the decisions that may be taken by the Committee.

(b) The decisions of the Committee are taken unanimously.

(c) When the Committee cannot reach a decision or deems it preferable to abstain, it transfers the case to the next Plenary Session, making any suggestions it deems appropriate.

(d) The Committee's decisions are brought to the notice of the Court at its next Plenary Session.

Article 5
Court Secretariat

1. In case of absence, the Secretary General may delegate to the General Counsel and Deputy Secretary General the authority to confirm arbitrators, to certify true copies of awards and to request the payment of a provisional advance, respectively provided for in Articles 9(2), 28(2) and 30(1) of the Rules.

2. The Secretariat may, with the approval of the Court, issue notes and other documents for the information of the parties and the arbitrators, or as necessary for the proper conduct of the arbitral proceedings.

Article 6
Scrutiny of Arbitral Awards

When the Court scrutinizes draft awards in accordance with Article 27 of the Rules, it considers, to the extent practicable, the requirements of mandatory law at the place of arbitration.

APPENDIX III
ARBITRATION COSTS AND FEES

Article 1
Advance on Costs

1. Each request to commence an arbitration pursuant to the Rules must be accompanied by an advance payment of US $2,500 on the administrative expenses. Such payment is non-refundable, and shall be credited to the Claimant's portion of the advance on costs.

2. The provisional advance on costs fixed by the Secretary General according to Article 30(1) of the Rules shall normally not exceed the amount obtained by adding together the administrative expenses, the minimum of the fees (as set out in the scale hereinafter) based upon the amount of the claim and the expected reimbursable expenses of the Arbitral Tribunal incurred with respect to the drafting of the Terms of Reference. If such amount is not quantified, the provisional advance shall be fixed at the discretion of the Secretary General. Payment by the Claimant shall be credited to its share of the advance on costs fixed by the Court.

3. In general, after the Terms of Reference have been signed or approved by the Court and the provisional timetable has been established, the Arbitral Tribunal shall, in accordance with Article 30(4) of the Rules, proceed only with respect to those claims or counterclaims in regard to which the whole of the advance on costs has been paid.

4. The advance on costs fixed by the Court according to Article 30(2) of the Rules comprises the fees of the arbitrator or arbitrators (hereinafter referred to as "arbitrator"), any arbitration-related expenses of the arbitrator and the administrative expenses.

5. Each party shall pay in cash its share of the total advance on costs. However, if its share exceeds an amount fixed from time to time by the Court, a party may post a bank guarantee for this additional amount.

6. A party that has already paid in full its share of the advance on costs fixed by the Court may, in accordance with Article 30(3) of the Rules, pay the unpaid portion of the advance owed by the defaulting party by posting a bank guarantee.

7. When the Court has fixed separate advances on costs pursuant to Article 30(2) of the Rules, the Secretariat shall invite each party to pay the amount of the advance corresponding to its respective claims.

8. When, as a result of the fixing of separate advances on costs, the separate advance fixed for the claim of either party exceeds one-half of such global advance as was previously fixed (in respect of the same claims and counterclaims that are the object of separate advances), a bank guarantee may be posted to cover

any such excess amount. In the event that the amount of the separate advance is subsequently increased, at least one-half of the increase shall be paid in cash.

9. The Secretariat shall establish the terms governing all bank guarantees which the parties may post pursuant to the above provisions.

10. As provided in Article 30(2) of the Rules, the advance on costs may be subject to readjustment at any time during the arbitration, in particular to take into account fluctuations in the amount in dispute, changes in the amount of the estimated expenses of the arbitrator or the evolving difficulty or complexity of arbitration proceedings.

11. Before any expertise ordered by the Arbitral Tribunal can be commenced, the parties, or one of them, shall pay an advance on costs fixed by the Arbitral Tribunal sufficient to cover the expected fees and expenses of the expert as determined by the Arbitral Tribunal. The Arbitral Tribunal shall be responsible for ensuring the payment by the parties of such fees and expenses.

Article 2
Costs and Fees

1. Subject to Article 31(2) of the Rules, the Court shall fix the fees of the arbitrator in accordance with the scale hereinafter set out or, where the sum in dispute is not stated, at its discretion.

2. In setting the arbitrator's fees, the Court shall take into consideration the diligence of the arbitrator, the time spent, the rapidity of the proceedings, and the complexity of the dispute so as to arrive at a figure within the limits specified, or, in exceptional circumstances (Article 31(2) of the Rules), at a figure higher or lower than those limits.

3. When a case is submitted to more than one arbitrator, the Court, at its discretion, shall have the right to increase the total fees up to a maximum which shall normally not exceed three times the fee of one arbitrator.

4. The Arbitrator's fees and expenses shall be fixed exclusively by the Court as required by the Rules. Separate fee arrangements between the parties and the arbitrators are contrary to the Rules.

5. The Court shall fix the administrative expenses of each arbitration in accordance with the scale hereinafter set out, or, where the sum in dispute is not stated, at its discretion. In exceptional circumstances, the Court may fix the administrative expenses at a lower or higher figure than that which would result from the application of such scale, provided that such expenses shall normally not exceed the maximum amount of the scale. Further, the Court may require the payment of administrative expenses in addition to those provided in the scale of administrative expenses as a condition to holding an arbitration in abeyance at the request of the parties or of one of them with the acquiescence of the other.

6. If an arbitration terminates before the rendering of a final award, the Court shall fix the costs of the arbitration at its discretion, taking into account the stage attained by the arbitral proceedings and any other relevant circumstances.

7. In the case of an application under Article 29(2) of the Rules, the Court may fix an advance to cover additional fees and expenses of the Arbitral Tribunal and may subordinate the transmission of such application to the Arbitral Tribunal to the prior cash payment in full to the ICC of such advance. The Court shall fix at its discretion any possible fees of the arbitrator when approving the decision of the Arbitral Tribunal.

8. When an arbitration is preceded by attempted conciliation, one-half of the administrative expenses paid for such conciliation shall be credited to the administrative expenses of the arbitration.

9. Amounts paid to the arbitrator do not include any possible value-added taxes (VAT) or other taxes or charges and imposts applicable to arbitrator's fees. Parties are expected to pay any such taxes or charges; however, the recovery of any such charges or taxes is a matter solely between the arbitrator and the parties.

Article 3
Appointment of Arbitrators

1. A registration fee normally not exceeding US $2,500 is payable by the requesting party in respect of each request made to the ICC to appoint an arbitrator for any arbitration not conducted under the Rules. No request for appointment of an arbitrator will be considered unless accompanied by the said fee, which is not recoverable and becomes the property of the ICC.

2. The said fee shall cover any additional services rendered by the ICC regarding the appointment, such as decisions on a challenge of an arbitrator and the appointment of a substitute arbitrator.

Article 4
Scales of Administrative Expenses
and of Arbitrator's Fees

1. The Scales of Administrative Expenses and Arbitrator's Fees set forth below shall be effective as of January 1,1998 in respect of all arbitrations commenced on or after such date, irrespective of the version of the Rules applying to such arbitrations.

2. To calculate the administrative expense and the arbitrator's fees, the amounts calculated for each successive slice of the sum in dispute must be added together, except that where the sum in dispute is over US$ 80 million, a flat amount of US$ 75,800 shall constitute the entirety of the administrative expenses.

A. Administrative Expenses

Sum in dispute (in US Dollars)				Admnistrative expenses (*)	
up to	50 000				$ 2 500
from	50 001	to	100 000		3.50%
from	1 00 001	to	500 000		1.70%
from	500 001	to	1 000 000		1.15%
from	1 000 001	to	2 000 0000		.60%
from	2 000 001	to	5 000 0000		.20%
from	5 000 001	to	10 000 0000		.10%
from	10 000 001	to	50 000 0000		.06%
from	50 000 001	to	80 000 0000		.06%
over	80 000 000				$ 75 800

(*) *For illustrative purposes only, the table on the following page indicates the resulting administrative expenses in US$ when the proper calculations have been made.*

B. Arbitrator's Fees

Sum in dispute (in US Dollars)				Fees(**)	
				minimum	maximum
up to	50 000			$ 2 500	17.00%
from	50 001	to	100 000	2.00%	11.00%
from	100 001	to	500 000	1.00%	5.50%
from	500 001	to	1 000 0000	0.75%	3.50%
from	1 000 001	to	2 000 0000	0.50%	2.50%
from	2 000 001	to	5 000 0000	0.25%	1.00%
from	5 000 001	to	10 000 0000	.10%	0.55%
from	10 000 001	to	50 000 0000	.05%	0.17%
from	50 000 001	to	80 000 0000	.03%	0.12%
from	80 000 001	to	100 000 0000	.02%	0.10%
over	100 000 0000			.01%	0.05%

(**) *For illustrative purposes only, the table on the following page indicates the resulting range of fees when the proper calculations have been made.*

Illustrative Calculation of Administrative Expenses and Arbitrator's Fees

Sum in dispute (in US Dollars)	A. Administrative Expenses(*) (in US Dollars)	B. Arbitrator's Fees(**) (in US Dollars) Minimum	B. Arbitrator's Fees(**) (in US Dollars) Maximum
Up to 50,000	2,500	2,500	17.00% of amt. in dispute
from 50,000 to 100,000	2,500+3.5% of amt. over 50,000	2,500+2.00% of amt. over 50,000	8,500+11.00% of amt. over 50,000
from 100,001 to 500,000	4,250+1.70% of amt. over 100,000	3,500+1.00% of amt. over 100,000	14,000+5.50% of amt. over 100,000
from 500,001 to 1,000,000	11,050+1.15% of amt. over 500,000	7,500+0.75% of amt. over 500,000	36,000+3.50% of amt. over 500,000
from 1,000,001 to 2,000,000	16,800+0.60% of amt. over 1,000,000	11,250+0.50% of amt. over 1,000,000	53,500+2.50% of amt. over 1,000,000
from 2,000,001 to 5,000,000	22,800+0.020% of amt. over 2,000,000	16,250+0.25% of amt. over 2,000,000	78,500+1.00% of amt. over 2,000,000
from 5,000,001 to 10,000,000	28,800+0.10% of amt. over 5,000,000	23,750+0.10% of amt. over 5,000,000	108,500+0.55% of amt. over 5,000,000
from 10,000,001 to 50,000,000	33,800+0.06% of amt. over 10,000,000	28,750+0.05% of amt. over 10,000,000	136,000+0.17% of amt. over 10,000,000
from 50,000,001 to 80,000,000	57,800+0.60% of amt. over 50,000,000	48,750+0.03% of amt. over 50,000,000	204,000+0.12% of amt. over 50,000,000
from 80,000,001 to 100,000,000	75,800	57,750+0.02% of amt. over 80,000,000	240,000+0.10% of amt. over 80,000,000
over 100,000,000	75,800	61,750+0.01% of amt. over 100,000,000	260,000+0.05% of amt. over 100,000,000

(*)(**) See Preceding page

INDEX

*"**AR**" refers to the Arbitration Rules of the International Chamber of Commerce*

*"**S**" refers to the Statutes of the International Court of Arbitration (Appendix I to the Rules)*

*"**IR**" refers to the Internal Rules of the Court (Appendix II to the Rules)*

*"**C**" refers to the Schedule of Costs applicable under the Rules (Appendix III to the Rules)*

Advance on Costs (See also "COSTS")

Bank guarantees, when and to what extent acceptable in payment of, C 1(5) (6) (9)

Cash, party's share of total advance payable in, C 1(5)

Court, determination of amount by, AR 30(2), C 1(4)

Expertise, additional advance on costs for, C 1(11)

Generally, AR 30

Non payment of, Arbitral Tribunal not to proceed after signature of Terms of Reference on claims or counterclaims for which advance not paid, C 1(3).

Provisional advance to be paid by Claimant, AR 30(1); amount of, C 1(2)

Readjustment of, C 1(10)

Secretary General, power to fix provisional advance, AR 30(1)

Separate advances for claims and counterclaims, AR 30(2), C 1(7) (8)

Advance Payment on Administrative Expense

Amount of, C 1(1)

Request for Arbitration to be accompanied by AR 4(4)

Agreement to Arbitrate

Court to be satisfied *prima facie* of existence of as condition for arbitration to proceed, AR 6(2)

Effect of, AR 6

Rules in effect on date of, AR 6(1)

Severability of agreement to arbitrate from contract in which it is found, AR 6(4)

Amiable Compositeur

Tribunal's powers, AR 17(3)

Annotated Guide to the 1998 ICC Arbitration Rules

Confidential character of the work of the International Court of Arbitration, IR 1(1) - 1(5) S6

Arbitral Tribunal's power to take measures concerning confidential information, AR 20(7)

National Committee, Court Members duty of confidentiality of Court proceedings in respect to, IR 3(1)(2)

Privacy of hearings, AR 21(3)

Privacy of session of International Court of Arbitration, IR 1(1)(2)

Conservatory and Interim Measures

Arbitral Tribunal, powers of, AR 23(1)

Judicial determination, AR 23(2)

Generally, AR 23

Security for, AR 23(1)

Consolidation

Powers of Court, AR 4(6)

Power of Arbitral Tribunal, AR 4(6)

Correction of Award (*See* "Award")

Costs (See also "Advance on Costs")

Calculation of, C 4

Correction and interpretation of awards, C 2(7)

Conciliation, credit for one-half of each administrative expense paid, C 2(8)

Defined, AR 31(1)

Determination in accordance with scale, C 2(5)

Discretion of Court, AR 31(2), C(2)(3)(5)(6)

Generally, AR 31, C 2

Court determination of, AR 31(1)(2)

Scale of, C 4

Separate fee arrangements agreed by parties forbidden, C 2(4)

Value added tax, C 2(9)

Counterclaim

Contents, AR 5(5)

Time for making, AR 5(5)

Reply to, by Claimant, AR 5(6)

Court of Arbitration (*See* "ICC International Court of Arbitration")

Date (*See* "Calculation of Time", "Time")

Default

Default of party arbitrator, appointment by court (where party defaults in nominating), AR 9(6)

Arbitration to proceed notwithstanding default of party, AR 6(3)

Hearing to proceed in absence of party duly summoned, AR 21(2)

Defense, Rights of (*See* "Due Process")

Documents

Retention in archive of Court of awards, terms of reference and decisions of Court, IR 1(6)

Due Process

Advisers, party's right to be assisted by, AR 21(4)

Arbitral Tribunal to act fairly and impartially, AR 15(2)

Generally, AR 35

Party to have reasonable opportunity to present its case, AR 15(2), 22(1)

Party's right to be heard in person, AR 20(2)

Party's right to be present at hearings, AR 21(3)

Reasonable notice of hearings to be given by Arbitral Tribunal, AR 21(1)

Exclusion of Liability

Arbitrators, AR 34

Court, AR 34

ICC, employees and National Committees, AR 34

Expert

Appointed by party, AR 20(3)

Appointed by Tribunal, AR 20(4)

Fair Hearing (*See* "Due Process")

Hearings

Arbitral Tribunal to be in full charge of, AR 21(3)

Notice of, by Arbitral Tribunal, AR 21(1)

Ordered by Tribunal, AR 20(2)

ICC International Court of Arbitration

Advance on costs, determination by, AR 30

Appointment of Chairman, Vice Chairman, S 3 (1)(2)

Appointment of Members of Court, AR 1(1), S 3(3)(4)(5)

Arbitral tribunal, decision on number of arbitrators, AR 8(2)

Arbitration Agreement, Court to be *prima facie* satisfied of existence of as condition for arbitration to proceed, AR 6(2)

Arbitrator, decisions by Court of appointment to confirmation, AR 7(4), 8(4), 9(1)(3)(4)

Arbitrator, decisions by Court of challenge or replacement of, AR 7(4), 11(3), 12, 12(5)

Chairman of the Court, AR 1(3), See also CHAIRMAN OF THE COURT

Committee of the Court, AR 1(4), S 5, IR 4

Composition of the Court, S 2

Costs, determination by AR 31(1)(2)

Documents, retention in archives of Court of awards, terms of reference and decisions of Court, IR 1(6)

Function, AR 1(1), S 1(1)

Internal Rules, AR 1(2)

Members of the Court, See MEMBERS OF THE COURT ·

National Committee, choice of to propose sole arbitrator or chairman, AR 9(3)

Plenary Session of Court, S 4

Quorum of Committee of Court, IR 4(4)

Quorum of Plenary Session, S 4

Secretariat of, AR 1(5)

Scrutiny of Awards, AR 27

Time limit shortened by parties' agreement, power of extension, AR 32(2)

Time limit for award, extensions of, AR 24(2)

Vice Chairman of the Court, See VICE CHAIRMAN OF THE COURT

International Court of Arbitration (*See* "ICC International Court of Arbitration")

Interpretation of Award (*See* "Award")

Members of The Court

Duty to advise Court of any involvement in ICC arbitration, IR 2(3)

Non-participation in Court proceeding when involved in any arbitration proceeding being considered, IR 2(4)(5)

National Committees, duty of confidentiality of Court proceedings in respect to, IR 3

Multiple Parties

Joint nomination by multiple Claimants or multiple Respondents of arbitrator for three person tribunal, AR 10(1)

Powers of Court in respect to appointment of arbitrators where multiple parties fail to agree on appointment, AR 10(2)

National Committees

Proposal of sole arbitrator or chairman for appointment by Court, AR 9(3)

Place of Arbitration

Agreed by parties, AR 14(1)

Award deemed made at, AR 25(3)

Fixed by Court, AR 14(1)

Deliberations by arbitrators at other locations, AR 14(3)

Hearings and meetings at other locations, AR 14(2)

Prima Facie Evidence of Arbitration Agreement

Court to be satisfied *prima facie* of existence of agreement to arbitrate, AR6(2).

Privacy (*See* "Confidentiality")

Hearings before Arbitral Tribunal, persons not involved in proceedings not to be admitted,

AR 21(3)

Session of International Court of Arbitration, open only to members and Secretariat, exceptions, IR 1(1)(2)

Registration Fee (*See* "Advance Payment on Administrative Expense")

Appointment by ICC of arbitrator for non-ICC arbitration, C 3

Replacement of Arbitrator

Grounds for, AR 12(1)(2)

Procedure for, AR 12(3)